The Missouri Drivers Permit Study Book 2025

Everything You Need to Pass the Missouri Permit Test on Your First Try!

Jonathan R. Edwards

The Missouri Drivers Permit Study Book 2025

DISCLAIMER

While every precaution has been taken in the preparation of this book, the publisher assumes no responsibility for errors or omissions, or for damages resulting from the use of the information contained herein.

The Missouri Drivers Permit Study Book 2025: Everything You Need to Pass the Missouri Permit Test on Your First Try!

First edition.

The Missouri Drivers Permit Study Book 2025

COPYRIGHT © JONATHAN R. EDWARDS 2025. ALL RIGHTS RESERVED

Before this document can be legally duplicated or reproduced in any manner, the publisher's consent must be gained. Therefore, the contents within this document can neither be stored electronically, transferred, nor kept in a database. Neither in part, nor in full can this document be copied, scanned, faxed, or retained without approval from the publisher or creator.

The Missouri Drivers Permit Study Book 2025

TABLE OF CONTENTS

Disclaimer 2

Copyright © Jonathan R. Edwards 2025. All Rights Reserved 3

Table of Contents 4

Chapter 1 7

   Introduction to the Missouri Driver's Permit 7

      1.1 Understanding the Missouri Graduated Driver License (GDL) Program 7

      1.2 Eligibility Requirements for a Missouri Learner's Permit 8

      1.3 Application Process and Required Documentation 10

      1.4 Overview of the Written Knowledge Test 13

Chapter 2 16

   Missouri Traffic Laws and Regulations 16

      2.1 Right-of-Way Rules and Intersections 16

      2.2 Speed Limits and Safe Driving Speeds 18

      2.3 Seat Belt and Child Restraint Laws 20

      2.4 Driving Under the Influence (DUI) Regulations 22

      2.5 Cell Phone Use and Texting While Driving 25

Chapter 3 28

   Road Signs and Traffic Signals 28

      3.1 Regulatory Signs and Their Meanings 28

      3.2 WARNING SIGNS: WHAT TO WATCH OUT FOR 31

      3.3 GUIDE SIGNS AND INFORMATION FOR DRIVERS 37

      3.4 Traffic Signals and Pavement Markings 42

Chapter 4 47

   Safe Driving Practices 47

      4.1 Defensive Driving Techniques 47

      4.2 Sharing the Road with Pedestrians and Cyclists 49

      4.3 Adjusting to Weather and Road Conditions 52

      4.4 Managing Driver Fatigue and Distractions 54

      4.5 Handling Emergencies and Breakdowns 56

The Missouri Drivers Permit Study Book 2025

Chapter 5 60
Vehicle Control and Operation 60
5.1 Basic Vehicle Controls and Instrumentation 60
5.2 Steering Techniques and Hand Positions 62
5.3 Acceleration, Braking, and Stopping Distances 65
5.4 Parking Methods: Parallel, Perpendicular, and Angle 67

Chapter 6 70
Missouri's Roadway Environments 70
6.1 Urban Driving: Navigating City Streets 70
6.2 Rural Driving: Challenges of Country Roads 72
6.3 Highway and Interstate Driving 75
6.4 Construction Zones and Work Areas 77

Chapter 7 81
Special Driving Situations 81
7.1 Night Driving: Visibility and Safety Tips 81
7.2 Driving in Adverse Weather Conditions 83
7.3 Mountain and Hill Driving Considerations 85
7.4 Navigating Missouri's Roundabouts and Traffic Circles 87

Chapter 8 90
Practice Tests and Study Resources 90
8.1 Practice Test 1 90
8.2 Practice Test 2 95
8.3 Practice Test 3 100
8.4 Practice Test 4 105
8.5 Practice Test 5 112
8.6 Long Practice Test 119
8.7 Tips for Effective Studying and Test-Taking 146
8.8 Additional Resources and Where to Find Them 148

The Missouri Drivers Permit Study Book 2025

CHAPTER 1
INTRODUCTION TO THE MISSOURI DRIVER'S PERMIT

1.1 UNDERSTANDING THE MISSOURI GRADUATED DRIVER LICENSE (GDL) PROGRAM

Navigating the journey to becoming a licensed driver in Missouri involves understanding the *Graduated Driver License (GDL) program*, a system designed to ensure that new drivers gain the necessary experience under conditions that minimize risk. This program introduces driving privileges in phases, allowing you to build skills and confidence before obtaining full driving rights.

Phase One: Instruction Permit

Your first step begins at age 15 with the **Instruction Permit**. To acquire this permit, you must pass vision, road sign recognition, and written knowledge tests at a Missouri State Highway Patrol examination station. After successfully completing these tests, visit a license office with a parent or legal guardian to obtain the actual permit; the test paper alone isn't valid for driving.

With this permit, if you're under 16, you may drive only when accompanied in the front seat by a qualified person—a parent, legal guardian, grandparent, qualified driving instructor, or an individual at least 25 years old with a valid license for a minimum of three years and written permission from your parent or guardian. Once you turn 16, the accompanying driver must be at least 21 years old with a valid license. Regardless of age, all passengers must wear seat belts, and you are prohibited from texting while driving.

Phase Two: Intermediate License

At 16, having held your Instruction Permit for at least six months and completed 40 hours of supervised driving (including 10 hours at night), you're eligible for the **Intermediate License**. This phase allows unsupervised driving with certain restrictions to ensure safety. For the first six months, you're limited to one passenger under 19 who isn't an immediate family member. After this period, you may carry up to three such passengers. Driving between 1 a.m. and 5 a.m. is restricted unless traveling to or from a school activity, job, or emergency, unless accompanied by a licensed driver 21 or older. Seat belts are mandatory for all occupants, and the prohibition on texting while driving continues.

Phase Three: Under-21 Full Driver License

Upon reaching 18, having held the Intermediate License without any alcohol-related offenses or traffic convictions in the preceding 12 months, you can graduate to the **Under-21 Full Driver License**. This license removes the passenger and nighttime driving restrictions, granting full driving privileges. However, adherence to all traffic laws, including seat belt use and the ban on texting while driving, remains crucial.

Parental Involvement and Responsibilities

Your parent or guardian plays a pivotal role throughout the GDL process. They must accompany you to the license office to sign your permit and license applications, certifying your completion of required supervised driving hours. They also have the authority to deny or reinstate your driving privileges if they believe it's necessary. Engaging in open discussions with them about safe driving practices and establishing a parent/teen driving agreement can further enhance your safety on the road.

Why the GDL Program Matters

The GDL program addresses the leading causes of teen driving incidents: inexperience, nighttime driving, and driving with passengers. By gradually introducing driving privileges, it allows you to gain experience in low-risk environments before facing more challenging driving situations. Research indicates that such programs can reduce teen driver crashes by 20 to 40 percent, underscoring the importance of adhering to each phase's requirements and restrictions.

Additional Considerations

While the GDL program sets the minimum standards, it's advisable to exceed these requirements to ensure your safety and that of others. This might include additional supervised driving hours, enrolling in defensive driving courses, and setting personal restrictions on nighttime driving and passenger numbers beyond those mandated.

Embarking on the path to becoming a licensed driver is both exciting and a significant responsibility. By understanding and adhering to Missouri's GDL program, you lay the foundation for a lifetime of safe and responsible driving.

1.2 ELIGIBILITY REQUIREMENTS FOR A MISSOURI LEARNER'S PERMIT

Embarking on the journey to obtain your *Missouri learner's permit* is a significant milestone, marking the beginning of your path toward responsible and skilled driving. Understanding the specific eligibility requirements is crucial to navigate this process smoothly and ensure you're well-prepared for the responsibilities that come with being a new driver.

Age Requirement

In Missouri, you must be at least *15 years old* to apply for an instruction permit. This age requirement aligns with the state's commitment to gradually introduce young drivers to the road, allowing them to gain experience under supervised conditions before advancing to more independent driving stages.

Parental or Guardian Consent

As a minor, obtaining consent from your parent or legal guardian is a mandatory step in the application process. They play an integral role not only in granting permission but also in accompanying you to the license office to sign the application. This involvement underscores the collaborative effort required to ensure your readiness and safety as a new driver.

Knowledge and Vision Examinations

Before applying for your permit, you must successfully pass several examinations administered by the Missouri State Highway Patrol (MSHP). These include:

- **Vision Test:** Assesses your visual acuity to ensure you can see clearly while driving.
- **Road Sign Recognition Test:** Evaluates your ability to recognize and understand various traffic signs, which is essential for safe navigation on the roads.
- **Written Knowledge Test:** Consists of 25 multiple-choice questions covering Missouri traffic laws, safe driving practices, and road sign meanings. A minimum score of 80% (answering at least 20 questions correctly) is required to pass.

Required Documentation

When visiting the license office to apply for your instruction permit, you'll need to present specific documents to verify your identity and residency. These include:

- **Proof of Identity and Lawful Status:** An original certified U.S. birth certificate or a valid U.S. passport.
- **Social Security Number Verification:** Your Social Security card.
- **Missouri Residency Proof:** Documents such as a bank statement, utility bill, or school transcript that include your name and current address.

Ensuring you have these documents ready will facilitate a smooth application process.

Application Process

The application process involves several steps:

1. **Testing:** Visit an MSHP examination station to complete the required vision, road sign recognition, and written knowledge tests.
2. **Documentation:** Gather all necessary documents verifying your identity, Social Security number, and Missouri residency.
3. **License Office Visit:** Accompanied by your parent or legal guardian, submit your documents and test results at a Missouri license office.
4. **Fee Payment:** Pay the $7.00 fee for the instruction permit.

Successfully completing these steps will grant you an instruction permit valid for 12 months, allowing you to begin supervised driving practice.

Supervised Driving Requirements

With your instruction permit, you're required to complete **40 hours of supervised driving**, including **10 hours of nighttime driving** between sunset and sunrise. These hours must be logged and verified by your supervising driver, typically your parent or legal guardian. This supervised practice is designed to provide you with diverse driving experiences under various conditions, building your confidence and competence behind the wheel.

Permit Restrictions

While holding an instruction permit, certain restrictions apply to ensure safety:

- **Supervising Driver:** If you're under 16, you may only drive when accompanied in the front seat by a qualified person—such as a parent, legal guardian, grandparent, qualified driving instructor, or an individual at least 25 years old with a valid license for a minimum of three years and written permission from your parent or guardian. Once you turn 16, the accompanying driver must be at least 21 years old with a valid license.
- **Seat Belts:** All occupants must wear seat belts at all times.
- **Electronic Devices:** The use of cell phones or any electronic communication devices while driving is prohibited.

Adhering to these restrictions is vital for your safety and the safety of others on the road.

Renewal and Validity

Your instruction permit is valid for 12 months and can be renewed if additional practice time is needed. If you lose your permit, you must apply for a duplicate by providing proof of identity and Missouri residency at any license office. Keeping your permit valid and in your possession is essential as you work toward obtaining your intermediate license.

Embarking on the path to becoming a licensed driver in Missouri requires diligence, responsibility, and a thorough understanding of the eligibility requirements for obtaining a learner's permit. By meeting these criteria and committing to the supervised practice, you lay a solid foundation for a lifetime of safe and responsible driving.

1.3 APPLICATION PROCESS AND REQUIRED DOCUMENTATION

Embarking on the journey to obtain your *Missouri instruction permit* is an exciting and pivotal step toward becoming a licensed driver. To navigate this process smoothly, it's essential to understand the detailed application procedures and gather all necessary documentation. This comprehensive guide will walk you through each stage, ensuring you're well-prepared to embark on your driving journey in Missouri.

Preparation Before the Application

Before initiating the application process, it's crucial to lay the groundwork to ensure a seamless experience. Begin by familiarizing yourself with the *Missouri Driver Guide*, which provides in-depth information on traffic laws, road signs, and safe driving practices specific to Missouri. Studying this guide thoroughly will equip you with the knowledge needed to excel in the written examination.

Additionally, ensure you meet the eligibility criteria:

- **Age Requirement:** You must be at least *15 years old* to apply for an instruction permit in Missouri.
- **Parental or Guardian Consent:** As a minor, obtaining consent from your parent or legal guardian is mandatory. They will need to accompany you during the application process to provide their approval.

Step 1: Visit a Missouri State Highway Patrol (MSHP) Examination Station

Your first actionable step is to visit an MSHP examination station to undertake the required tests. These stations are strategically located throughout the state, and you can find the nearest one by visiting the Missouri State Highway Patrol's official website.

At the examination station, you will undergo the following assessments:

- **Vision Test:** This evaluates your visual acuity to ensure you can see clearly while driving. Adequate vision is paramount for identifying road signs, pedestrians, and other vehicles.
- **Road Sign Recognition Test:** You'll be tested on your ability to recognize and understand various traffic signs. This ensures you can interpret essential information while on the road.
- **Written Knowledge Test:** This multiple-choice exam assesses your understanding of Missouri's traffic laws, safe driving practices, and road sign meanings. A passing score requires correctly answering at least 20 out of 25 questions, equating to an 80% success rate.

Step 2: Obtain the Driver Examination Record (Form DOR-100)

Upon successfully completing the tests at the MSHP examination station, you will receive a *Driver Examination Record* (Form DOR-100). This document serves as official proof of your test results and is a prerequisite for the next phase of the application process.

Step 3: Gather Required Documentation

Before heading to the license office, compile all necessary documents to verify your identity, lawful status, Social Security number, and Missouri residency. Having these documents organized and ready will expedite the application process.

Proof of Identity and Lawful Status:

To establish your identity and lawful presence in the United States, present one of the following:

- *Original certified U.S. birth certificate* issued by a vital records agency.
- Valid, unexpired U.S. passport.
- Certificate of Citizenship or Naturalization.

Ensure that all documents are original or certified copies; photocopies or notarized copies are not acceptable.

Proof of Social Security Number:

Provide your *Social Security card*, which must be:

- Signed if you are 18 years of age or older.
- Unlaminated.

If you do not have a Social Security number, you must present a letter from the Social Security Administration indicating your ineligibility.

Proof of Missouri Residential Address:

To verify your Missouri residency, present documents that include your name and current residential address. Acceptable examples include:

- *Recent utility bill* (e.g., water, gas, electric) dated within the last 60 days.
- *Bank statement* issued within the last 60 days.
- *Paycheck stub* dated within the last 60 days.

If you are applying for a *REAL ID-compliant* permit, you must provide two documents from different sources to establish residency.

Additional Documentation for Name Changes:

If your current legal name differs from the name on your identity documents, due to marriage, divorce, or other reasons, provide legal documentation of the name change, such as:

- Marriage certificate.
- Divorce decree.
- Court order approving the name change.

Step 4: Visit a Missouri License Office

With your Driver Examination Record and the required documents in hand, proceed to a Missouri license office to complete the application process. Your parent or legal guardian must accompany you to:

- Sign the application, providing consent for you to obtain the instruction permit.
- Certify that they will ensure you receive the required behind-the-wheel instruction.

At the license office, you will:

- Submit all gathered documentation.
- Complete the application form for a Missouri instruction permit.
- Pay the $7.00 fee for the instruction permit.

The license office personnel will process your application, verify your documents, and issue your instruction permit, which is valid for 12 months.

The Missouri Drivers Permit Study Book 2025

Understanding the REAL ID Act and Its Implications

Missouri offers both *REAL ID-compliant* and *non-REAL ID-compliant* permits. The REAL ID Act, established to enhance security standards for state-issued identification, affects the types of identification accepted for federal purposes, such as boarding domestic flights or entering federal facilities.

1.4 OVERVIEW OF THE WRITTEN KNOWLEDGE TEST

Taking the written knowledge test is a crucial step in obtaining your *Missouri instruction permit*, and understanding exactly what to expect can make all the difference in ensuring you pass on your first try. This test is designed to assess your knowledge of *Missouri traffic laws, road signs, and safe driving practices*. Since every question is based on real-life driving scenarios, getting familiar with the format, content, and best preparation strategies will help you feel confident when you sit for the test.

The test is administered at *Missouri State Highway Patrol (MSHP) examination stations* and is typically taken on a touchscreen computer. If you require special accommodations due to a disability or a language barrier, you can request assistance before starting. The exam consists of *25 multiple-choice questions*, and you must answer at least *20 correctly*—which is an *80% passing score*—to move forward in the licensing process. While that might sound manageable, underestimating the difficulty of the test could lead to failure, so preparing thoroughly is essential.

Each question on the test is carefully crafted to ensure that you understand *both the rules of the road and the reasoning behind them*. You won't just be asked to memorize speed limits or traffic signals; instead, you'll be tested on your ability to *apply* that knowledge in real-world situations. For example, rather than simply asking, "What is the speed limit in a residential area?" you may be presented with a question like:

A car is driving through a neighborhood where children are playing near the street. The driver is maintaining a speed of 30 mph. What should the driver do?

The multiple-choice answers would include:

A) Continue driving at 30 mph, since that is the speed limit.
B) Increase speed to pass through the area quickly.
C) Slow down and be prepared to stop.
D) Honk to alert the children of the car's presence.

If you've studied thoroughly, you'd recognize that the correct answer is *C: Slow down and be prepared to stop*. Even if the posted speed limit is 30 mph, *Missouri law requires drivers to adjust their speed based on road conditions and potential hazards*. This is the kind of situational awareness the test is designed to measure, so simply memorizing laws won't be enough—you need to understand their application.

A major portion of the test focuses on *Missouri-specific traffic regulations*. While some laws are the same across the United States, others are unique to

Missouri, and you'll be expected to know them. For instance, Missouri is not a "hands-free" state, which means that although texting while driving is illegal for drivers under 21, it is technically legal for adult drivers to use handheld devices while behind the wheel. Another important law to remember is *Missouri's Move Over Law*, which requires you to *change lanes or slow down* when approaching emergency vehicles stopped on the roadside. Questions related to these laws may appear on the test, and failing to understand them could mean missing valuable points.

Another key part of the test involves *road signs and their meanings*. Some questions will show you an image of a sign and ask you to identify it, while others will describe a situation where you need to recognize which sign applies. You should be able to distinguish between *regulatory signs* (which tell you what you must or must not do, such as stop signs and speed limit signs), *warning signs* (which alert you to potential hazards like sharp curves or pedestrian crossings), and *guide signs* (which provide information about directions, distances, and services). Knowing the difference between a *yellow diamond-shaped sign* and a *white rectangular sign* can help you quickly determine what action to take when answering a question.

The test will also assess your understanding of *right-of-way rules*, which determine who has priority in different traffic situations. For example, you may encounter a question asking who has the right of way at a four-way stop when multiple cars arrive at the same time. To answer correctly, you'd need to recall that *the vehicle on the right has the right of way*, unless another driver is already in the intersection. You may also be tested on yielding to pedestrians, emergency vehicles, and school buses with flashing red lights—all of which are critical for safe driving.

A portion of the test will cover *defensive driving techniques*, which help reduce the risk of accidents. You'll be asked questions about following distance, stopping distance, and how to react in adverse conditions. For example, you might see a question like:

You are driving on a highway when heavy rain begins to fall. What is the safest action to take?

The answer choices could include:

A) Maintain the speed limit and use cruise control.
B) Turn on high beams for better visibility.
C) Slow down, increase your following distance, and use windshield wipers.
D) Speed up to reach your destination before the rain worsens.

The correct answer is *C: Slow down, increase your following distance, and use windshield wipers*, since wet roads can cause reduced traction and longer stopping distances. This type of question ensures that you understand not only what to do but why it's necessary for road safety.

Even though the test is not timed, it's best to pace yourself and read each question carefully. Some questions are worded in a way that may trick you if you rush. For example, a question might ask, "Which of the following is *not* a safe driving practice?" If you skim too quickly, you may overlook the word *not* and select an incorrect answer. Paying close attention to every detail will help prevent unnecessary mistakes.

One of the best ways to prepare for the test is by taking *Missouri permit practice tests*, which are available online and at some driver education centers. These practice tests simulate the real exam format and give you a chance to identify any weak areas. If you consistently struggle with questions about right-of-way or road signs, you'll know to spend extra time reviewing those sections in the *Missouri Driver Guide*.

Before test day, make sure to get a good night's sleep and eat a meal beforehand. Although the test itself isn't physically demanding, being well-rested and focused can help you think more clearly. When you arrive at the testing location, have all necessary documents with you, including proof of identity and your *Driver Examination Record* (Form DOR-100), which you received after completing the vision and road sign tests.

If you don't pass the test on your first attempt, don't be discouraged. Missouri allows you to retake the exam as soon as the next business day. However, if you fail three times, you will need to get special permission from the *Missouri Department of Revenue* before taking the test again. Rather than rushing to retake it, use the time to study the sections where you struggled so you can be fully prepared for the next attempt.

Passing the written knowledge test is an important milestone, as it demonstrates that you have the fundamental knowledge required to drive safely in Missouri. Once you pass, you'll receive your *instruction permit*, allowing you to begin gaining real-world driving experience under the supervision of a licensed adult. The more you practice and apply the concepts you've learned, the more confident and prepared you'll be when it's time for the next step: the road skills test.

The Missouri Drivers Permit Study Book 2025

CHAPTER 2
MISSOURI TRAFFIC LAWS AND REGULATIONS

2.1 RIGHT-OF-WAY RULES AND INTERSECTIONS

Understanding *right-of-way rules* is one of the most critical aspects of safe driving, especially at intersections where vehicles, pedestrians, and cyclists frequently cross paths. Failing to yield when required can lead to serious accidents, confusion on the road, and traffic violations. Knowing when to proceed and when to allow others to go first ensures that traffic flows smoothly and predictably, reducing the risk of collisions and keeping everyone safe.

At any intersection, the *right-of-way* is not something you take—it is something you give. The law does not grant you the right-of-way in a situation; it only states when you must yield to others. That means even if you technically have the right-of-way, it is always your responsibility to avoid a crash, even if another driver fails to follow the rules. This is why defensive driving is so important. Rather than assuming another driver will stop or yield, you should always be prepared to slow down or adjust your course if necessary.

Intersections come in different forms—some are controlled by *traffic signals or stop signs*, while others are completely *uncontrolled*, meaning no signs or signals dictate the flow of traffic. In Missouri, the rules vary depending on the type of intersection you are approaching, so knowing what to do in each scenario is essential. At *four-way stops*, also known as *all-way stops*, the rule is simple: the first vehicle to arrive at the intersection has the right-of-way. If two vehicles arrive at the same time, the driver on the *right* has the right-of-way. If you arrive at a four-way stop at the same time as another vehicle and you are to the *left*, you must allow the other driver to go first. If drivers approach from all directions at once, it is important to make eye contact and use hand signals when necessary to communicate intentions clearly.

At *two-way stops*, where only one direction of traffic has stop signs, the rule is different. Drivers at the stop sign must yield to *all* cross traffic before proceeding. If you are at a stop sign and another vehicle is traveling through the intersection on a road that does not have a stop sign, you must wait until it has passed before moving forward. If you are turning left across traffic at an intersection without signals, you must yield to *oncoming vehicles that are going straight* or turning right. This ensures that vehicles moving straight through the intersection do not have to stop suddenly for left-turning drivers, which could cause rear-end collisions.

Traffic signals control many intersections in Missouri, and while they provide clear guidance, it is still important to understand how right-of-way applies. A *green light* means you may proceed if the way is clear, but it does not automatically guarantee that all other drivers or pedestrians will follow their own signals. Before moving forward, always check that no vehicles are running a red light or turning unexpectedly. A *yellow light* warns that the signal is about to turn red, and unless it is unsafe to do so, you should stop rather than trying to speed through the intersection. A *red light* means you must stop completely and wait for the light to turn green before proceeding. If you are turning *right on red*, you must first come to a complete stop and check for traffic, then yield to *all cross traffic and pedestrians* before making your turn.

Left turns at traffic signals can be more complicated because the right-of-way depends on whether the signal provides a *protected* or *unprotected* turn. A *green arrow* means your turn is protected, and all oncoming traffic must stop. However, if you have a *solid green light* without an arrow, your left turn is *unprotected*, meaning you must yield to oncoming vehicles before turning. Many accidents happen when drivers fail to properly yield on unprotected left turns, so taking the time to ensure the way is clear is crucial.

Uncontrolled intersections, which are often found in residential areas or rural locations, can be the most unpredictable since there are no traffic lights or stop signs regulating who should go first. When approaching one, you must slow down and be prepared to yield if another vehicle is already in or near the intersection. If two vehicles arrive at an uncontrolled intersection at the same time, the driver on the right has the right-of-way. However, because not all drivers are familiar with this rule, it is always a good idea to *proceed cautiously, make eye contact with other drivers, and be prepared to stop if needed.*

Pedestrians and cyclists also play a role in right-of-way rules, and Missouri law requires drivers to *always* yield to pedestrians in crosswalks. If a pedestrian is crossing the street at a marked or unmarked crosswalk, you must stop and allow them to reach the other side safely. You must also stop for pedestrians crossing at intersections with traffic signals, even if your light is green, if they are still in the crosswalk. If a pedestrian is waiting to cross at an intersection without signals, you should slow down and prepare to stop to allow them to cross. It is also illegal to pass a vehicle that is stopped at a crosswalk, as they may be yielding to a pedestrian you cannot see.

School zones and pedestrian-heavy areas require even more caution. When driving through a school zone, Missouri law requires you to *reduce your speed and watch for children crossing the road*. Flashing yellow lights or posted signs indicate that you must slow down, and if a school crossing guard is present, you must always obey their instructions. Pedestrians, especially children, can be unpredictable, so it is crucial to be extra alert in these areas.

Emergency vehicles, including police cars, fire trucks, and ambulances, have special right-of-way rules in Missouri. If an emergency vehicle is approaching with its lights and sirens on, you must *pull over to the right side of the road and stop until it has passed*. This applies even if you are at an intersection—if you hear sirens while waiting at a red light, you should remain stopped and allow the emergency vehicle to maneuver around you. Missouri's *Move Over Law* also requires you to change lanes or slow down when approaching a stopped emergency vehicle on the side of the road. If it is unsafe to change lanes, you must *reduce your speed and proceed with caution.*

Railroad crossings also have their own right-of-way rules, and failing to follow them can be deadly. Trains *always* have the right-of-way, and Missouri law requires drivers to stop at *least 15 feet* from the tracks when a train is approaching. Flashing lights, lowered crossing gates, or a train horn indicate that a train is coming, and you must remain stopped until the train has completely cleared the crossing. It is illegal and extremely dangerous to drive around lowered gates or attempt to beat a train. Even if you do not see a train, always *look both ways before crossing* to ensure the tracks are clear.

Understanding and correctly following right-of-way rules is essential for safe driving, and knowing these rules will help you make quick, confident decisions on the road. Whether you are approaching an intersection, yielding to pedestrians, or responding to an emergency vehicle, remembering that *right-of-way is something you give, not take* will ensure that you remain a responsible and cautious driver.

2.2 SPEED LIMITS AND SAFE DRIVING SPEEDS

Speed limits are one of the most fundamental traffic laws designed to ensure safe and efficient travel. Whether you are driving through a bustling city, cruising down a quiet rural road, or navigating a major highway, Missouri has established *specific speed limits* that you are required to follow. These limits are determined based on factors such as road conditions, surrounding environments, and the likelihood of encountering pedestrians or other obstacles. However, simply obeying posted speed limits is not always enough to drive safely—you must also adjust your speed based on weather, traffic, and visibility conditions. Understanding when and why you should modify your speed, even when signs do not require it, is essential for responsible driving.

Missouri's *default speed limits* vary depending on the type of road you are driving on. If there are no posted signs, the general rules apply. On *interstate highways* and *rural expressways*, the maximum speed limit is usually *70 miles per hour*. This allows for faster travel between cities and across long stretches of open road. However, certain areas of the interstate may have *lower speed limits*, especially near cities or construction zones, where a high volume of vehicles or roadwork could increase the risk of accidents. *Urban highways and expressways* typically have a limit of *60 miles per hour*, while *state roads* that run through rural areas often allow speeds of up to *65 miles per hour*.

Within *city limits*, speed limits are lower because there are more pedestrians, intersections, and vehicles stopping or turning. The maximum speed on *most city streets* is *25 to 35 miles per hour*, but this can vary depending on local ordinances. Residential neighborhoods, school zones, and areas with high pedestrian traffic often have *even lower limits*, requiring you to slow down to keep people safe. School zones, in particular, are strictly enforced, with most areas limiting speeds to *20 miles per hour* during school hours. Flashing lights or posted signs will indicate when reduced speed limits are in effect, and failing to follow them can result in hefty fines and penalties.

One of the most misunderstood aspects of speed limits is the fact that they represent the *maximum legal speed under ideal conditions*. This means that even if a road is marked with a 70 mph speed limit, you are not always allowed—or expected—to drive at that speed. Missouri law states that drivers must *adjust their speed* based on current road and weather conditions. This is known as the *basic speed law*, which requires you to drive at a speed that is *reasonable and safe* for the conditions, regardless of the posted limit. For example, if it is raining heavily, the road is covered in ice, or there is thick fog reducing visibility, driving at the posted speed limit could still be dangerous.

Weather conditions play a significant role in determining a *safe driving speed*. Rain, snow, ice, and fog all create hazards that require you to slow down. Wet roads reduce traction, increasing the risk of hydroplaning—when your tyres lose contact with the road surface and cause you to lose control of your vehicle. If it has been raining for a while, oil and debris on the road can make conditions even more slippery. In icy or snowy conditions, slowing down significantly is crucial, as braking distances increase dramatically. Even if the road *looks* clear, black ice—an invisible, thin layer of ice—can make it nearly impossible to stop in time if you are driving too fast. Fog is another major hazard, as it reduces visibility and makes it difficult to judge the distance between your vehicle and others. If you cannot see more than a few feet ahead, reducing your speed and using your low-beam headlights is essential.

Traffic congestion is another factor that can affect safe driving speeds. Even if the speed limit is 60 mph on a highway, heavy traffic may make it unsafe to travel at that speed. If vehicles ahead of you are slowing down or stopping frequently, you must also reduce your speed to maintain a safe following distance. Sudden stops and lane changes are common in congested areas, and driving too fast increases the likelihood of rear-end collisions. Paying attention to the flow of traffic and adjusting your speed accordingly helps prevent accidents and ensures smoother travel.

Construction zones are another area where reduced speed limits are strictly enforced. Missouri has *specific laws* requiring drivers to *slow down and exercise extreme caution* when approaching and driving through construction areas. Speed limits in these zones are usually posted well in advance, and you should always be on the lookout for signs indicating changes in speed. Even if you do not see workers immediately, the road may have uneven surfaces, lane shifts, or unexpected obstacles that require you to slow down. In Missouri, fines for speeding in construction zones are significantly higher than standard speeding violations, especially when workers are present.

Missouri also enforces a *minimum speed limit* on highways to prevent slow-moving vehicles from disrupting the flow of traffic. On interstates where the maximum speed limit is 70 mph, the minimum speed is often set at *40 mph*. If you are driving too slowly and causing a hazard to other motorists, you may be pulled over for impeding traffic. However, if road conditions, vehicle malfunctions, or other factors make it unsafe to drive at the minimum speed, you should use your hazard lights and pull over if necessary until conditions improve.

Speeding violations in Missouri carry serious consequences, including fines, points on your driving record, and potential license suspension. If you are caught exceeding the speed limit, the penalty depends on how far over the limit you were driving. Generally, fines increase with the severity of the violation. If you are caught driving *5 to 10 mph over the speed limit*, you may receive a small fine, but if you are caught going *20 mph or more over the limit*, the penalties become much harsher. Repeated speeding violations can lead to the suspension of your driving privileges, and excessive speeding in a construction or school zone can result in additional penalties.

Beyond legal consequences, driving at unsafe speeds increases the risk of serious accidents. Studies have shown that *the faster a vehicle is traveling at the time of impact, the greater the force of the crash and the likelihood of severe injuries or fatalities*. High-speed collisions are more likely to result in loss of vehicle control, and when a crash occurs at excessive speeds, the ability of safety features like airbags and seatbelts to protect you is significantly reduced. This is why Missouri law requires you to not only follow posted speed limits but also drive at a speed that is *appropriate for the conditions around you*.

Safe driving is not just about obeying the law—it is about making decisions that protect you and others on the road. Recognizing when to slow down, staying aware of changes in road conditions, and respecting posted speed limits all contribute to a safer driving experience. Speed limits are not suggestions; they are carefully determined based on the specific needs of each road and the safety of all road users. By understanding how to adjust your speed responsibly, you will not only stay within the law but also reduce your risk of accidents and become a more confident, cautious driver.

2.3 SEAT BELT AND CHILD RESTRAINT LAWS

Seat belts are among the simplest yet most effective safety features in any vehicle, drastically reducing the risk of injury or death in the event of a crash. In Missouri, wearing a seat belt is not just a recommendation—it is a legal requirement for drivers and passengers. The law is clear about who must wear seat belts and when, and failing to comply can result in fines and penalties. However, beyond legal obligations, understanding the importance of seat belts can mean the difference between life and death in an accident. No matter how short the journey or how familiar the road, using a seat belt correctly should be second nature every time you get into a vehicle.

The Missouri seat belt law requires *all drivers and front-seat passengers* to wear seat belts at all times while the vehicle is in motion. Although passengers in the back seat are not legally required to wear seat belts in some circumstances, it is still highly recommended for safety. Research has consistently shown that unbelted passengers in the back seat are just as vulnerable to serious injuries in a crash and can even pose a risk to belted front-seat occupants if they are thrown forward during impact. A properly worn seat belt should go *across your shoulder and chest* rather than under your arm or behind your back, ensuring maximum protection. The lap belt should fit snugly across your hips and not rest on your stomach.

For drivers under the age of 16, Missouri has *specific requirements* that mandate seat belt use for all passengers, regardless of where they are sitting in the vehicle. This means that if you are transporting younger passengers, you are responsible for ensuring that they are properly restrained. Law enforcement officers have the right to stop a vehicle if they notice that a driver or front-seat passenger is not wearing a seat belt, as Missouri enforces seat belt laws through *secondary enforcement*—meaning that an officer must have another reason to pull you over before issuing a seat belt citation.

Wearing a seat belt significantly reduces the risk of ejection from a vehicle in a collision. Statistics show that in severe crashes, unbelted occupants are often thrown from the vehicle, leading to catastrophic injuries or fatalities. The force of impact in a collision can cause your body to move at the same speed your car was traveling, making it nearly impossible to brace for impact. Seat belts work by keeping you *securely in place*, preventing unnecessary movement that could result in injury. In addition, seat belts distribute the force of a crash across the *strongest parts of your body*—your chest, shoulders, and hips—rather than concentrating it in one vulnerable area.

Beyond seat belts, child restraint laws in Missouri are designed to offer additional protection for young passengers who are more vulnerable in accidents. The state has strict regulations regarding *child safety seats, booster seats, and seat belt use for minors* to ensure that children are properly secured based on their age, weight, and height. For infants and toddlers under the age of two, Missouri law requires that they be secured in a *rear-facing car seat*. These seats provide the best support for a baby's developing neck and spine by distributing the force of a crash evenly across the back of the seat rather than the child's body.

Once a child reaches the age of two or outgrows the weight and height limits for their rear-facing seat, they must transition to a *forward-facing car seat with a harness*. These seats provide added protection by keeping the child restrained in a way that prevents excessive forward movement in the event of a collision. The harness should always be positioned correctly over the child's shoulders and chest, and the seat itself must be properly secured to the vehicle using either the seat belt or the LATCH system.

For older children who have outgrown their forward-facing car seat but are not yet tall enough to use a seat belt alone, Missouri law requires the use of a *booster seat*. A booster seat helps position the seat belt correctly across a child's shoulder and lap, ensuring that it provides adequate protection in a crash. Children should remain in a booster seat until they are at least *eight years old or 80 pounds* in weight. However, experts recommend that children continue using a booster seat until they are *tall enough for the seat belt to fit properly*—typically around *4 feet 9 inches* in height.

Missouri law also states that *all children under the age of 16 must be properly restrained in a seat belt or child safety seat, regardless of where they are sitting in the vehicle.* If a child is under the age of *four*, they must be secured in an *appropriate child safety seat* at all times. For children between the ages of four and seven who weigh *less than 80 pounds* and are *shorter than 4 feet 9 inches*, the use of a *booster seat is mandatory*. However, if a child meets the height or weight requirements to use a seat belt without a booster seat, the seat belt must fit properly across their chest and hips.

Proper installation of child safety seats is crucial to their effectiveness. A car seat that is not installed correctly can fail to provide adequate protection in a crash. Missouri offers *inspection stations* where certified technicians can check your car seat installation free of charge, ensuring that it meets safety standards. Common mistakes include failing to tighten the seat belt or LATCH system properly, using the wrong harness slot for the child's height, or allowing too much movement in the seat. To ensure maximum safety, you should always follow the *manufacturer's guidelines* when installing a car seat and securing a child in place.

Failure to comply with Missouri's seat belt and child restraint laws can result in *fines, penalties, and even points on your driving record*. If you are caught driving without a seat belt or allowing a child to ride without proper restraints, you can be ticketed. The penalties for child restraint violations are often higher than those for adult seat belt infractions, as children are more vulnerable to serious injury in a crash. Beyond the legal consequences, failing to wear a seat belt or secure a child properly could result in devastating injuries or fatalities in the event of an accident.

It is important to recognize that seat belts and child restraints are not just about obeying the law—they are about protecting lives. Even at low speeds, an unrestrained passenger can be thrown forward with tremendous force, leading to life-threatening injuries. Airbags are not a substitute for seat belts, as they are designed to work together to reduce the impact of a crash. In fact, airbags can be dangerous if a passenger is not wearing a seat belt, as the force of deployment can cause serious harm to an unrestrained occupant.

Developing the habit of wearing a seat belt every time you get into a vehicle is one of the most effective ways to protect yourself. As a driver, you are also responsible for ensuring that your passengers are buckled up, especially children who rely on adults to keep them safe. Making seat belt use a non-negotiable rule for everyone in the car not only reduces the risk of injury but also sets an example for younger passengers who will one day be drivers themselves. Safe driving starts with the choices you make before you even start the engine, and buckling up is the first step to ensuring a safe journey.

2.4 DRIVING UNDER THE INFLUENCE (DUI) REGULATIONS

Driving under the influence is one of the most dangerous and strictly regulated offenses on the road. The effects of alcohol and drugs on your ability to operate a vehicle safely are severe, and Missouri law does not take violations lightly. Whether you are a first-time driver or someone with years of experience, understanding the legal limits, consequences, and risks associated with impaired driving is critical. Even the slightest impairment can make you a danger to yourself and others on the road, which is why law enforcement officers actively enforce DUI laws across the state.

In Missouri, it is illegal for you to operate a vehicle if your *blood alcohol concentration (BAC) is 0.08% or higher*. This is the standard legal limit for most drivers, but for those under the age of 21, the threshold is even stricter. If you are underage, you can be charged with a DUI if your BAC is *0.02% or higher*, even if you do not feel intoxicated. The law reflects the fact that alcohol affects everyone differently, and even a small amount can impair judgment, slow reaction times, and reduce coordination—all of which are essential for safe driving.

Law enforcement officers in Missouri use a variety of methods to determine whether a driver is under the influence. If you are pulled over on suspicion of impaired driving, the officer may ask you to perform *field sobriety tests*. These tests assess your balance, coordination, and ability to follow instructions—things that alcohol and drugs can quickly impair. A common test is the *horizontal gaze nystagmus test*, in which the officer will have you follow an object with your eyes to see if your pupils jerk involuntarily. Other tests include walking in a straight line, standing on one foot, and reciting the alphabet backward. Failing any of these could lead to further testing, such as a *breathalyzer test*, which measures your BAC by analyzing your breath. If you refuse to take a breathalyzer test, you may face *immediate consequences* under Missouri's *implied consent law*.

The implied consent law states that by obtaining a driver's license in Missouri, you have already agreed to submit to BAC testing if an officer has probable cause to believe you are under the influence. Refusing to take a breath, blood, or urine test when requested can result in *an automatic one-year driver's license suspension*, regardless of whether you were actually impaired. This administrative penalty is separate from any DUI charges you might face in court, meaning that refusing a test does not necessarily help you avoid legal trouble.

If you are convicted of a DUI in Missouri, the penalties vary depending on the circumstances. A *first-time offense* can lead to fines of up to $1,000, a license suspension of 90 days, and up to six months in jail. You may also be required to complete an alcohol education program and install an *ignition interlock device (IID)* in your vehicle, which prevents your car from starting unless you pass a breathalyzer test. A *second DUI offense* carries even harsher consequences, including up to one year in jail, fines of up to $2,000, and a *five-year license revocation* if the second offense occurs within five years of the first. If you are convicted *three or more times*, you may face felony charges, which come with even steeper fines, mandatory jail time, and long-term restrictions on your driving privileges.

Missouri also enforces strict DUI laws for drivers under the age of 21. Because underage drinking is illegal, any BAC of *0.02% or higher* can result in a DUI charge. This is known as the *Zero Tolerance Law*, and it means that even one drink could lead to serious legal consequences. A first offense under this law can result in a *90-day license suspension*, while multiple offenses can lead to *longer suspensions or even revocation*. Additionally, if you are under 21 and caught drinking and driving, you may face penalties beyond the DUI itself, including *community service, fines, and mandatory alcohol awareness programs.*

Drug-impaired driving is treated just as seriously as alcohol-impaired driving. Even if you have not consumed alcohol, you can still be arrested for DUI if you are under the influence of *illegal drugs, prescription medications, or over-the-counter drugs that impair your ability to drive safely.* Missouri law does not require a specific BAC limit for drug-related DUIs, meaning that if an officer determines that you are impaired, you can be arrested regardless of how much of a substance is in your system. This includes marijuana, even though medical marijuana is legal in Missouri. Having a medical marijuana card does not give you the right to drive while under the influence, and doing so can result in the same penalties as an alcohol-related DUI.

The impact of a DUI conviction goes beyond fines and jail time. A DUI can have long-term effects on your life, affecting your *insurance rates, employment opportunities, and ability to travel.* Many employers perform background checks, and having a DUI on your record can make it harder to get certain jobs. Your *car insurance premiums* will likely increase significantly, as insurance companies view DUI offenders as high-risk drivers. Some policies may even be canceled altogether, forcing you to seek expensive *high-risk insurance* to remain legally covered. Additionally, a DUI conviction can prevent you from entering certain countries, as some nations have strict entry restrictions for those with criminal records.

Law enforcement officers in Missouri conduct *sobriety checkpoints* to catch impaired drivers before they cause accidents. At these checkpoints, officers stop vehicles at random to check for signs of intoxication. If you are found to be under the influence at a checkpoint, you can be arrested on the spot. These checkpoints are legal and have been upheld by the courts as an effective tool for preventing DUI-related crashes.

The dangers of impaired driving cannot be overstated. Alcohol and drugs affect the brain in ways that make safe driving impossible. Reaction times slow down, making it harder to *brake in time to avoid a collision.* Judgment becomes impaired, leading to risky decisions such as *speeding, running red lights, or swerving into other lanes.* Vision can become blurry, and coordination suffers, making it difficult to control the vehicle. Most DUI-related crashes happen because the driver *underestimated how impaired they were*, believing they were still capable of driving safely when, in reality, they were not.

Every year, thousands of people are injured or killed in crashes caused by impaired drivers. The consequences of choosing to drive under the influence extend beyond legal penalties—they can result in *serious injury or death to you, your passengers, or innocent people on the road.* Many DUI-related accidents involve *head-on collisions, rollovers, or high-speed crashes*, all of which increase the likelihood of severe injuries or fatalities. Families are torn apart, and lives are changed forever, all because of a choice that could have been avoided.

There is never a safe amount of alcohol or drugs when it comes to driving. If you plan to drink, you should always have a *designated driver, use a rideshare service, or stay where you are until you are sober*. If you ever find yourself in a situation where you are too impaired to drive, asking for help is always the better option than risking a DUI—or worse, a fatal crash.

Choosing to drive sober is one of the most responsible decisions you can make. Not only does it keep you safe, but it also protects everyone else on the road. Whether you are a new driver or someone with experience, the message remains the same: *impaired driving is never worth the risk*.

2.5 CELL PHONE USE AND TEXTING WHILE DRIVING

Distractions while driving come in many forms, but few are as common or as dangerous as using a *cell phone* behind the wheel. Whether it is checking a message, scrolling through social media, or answering a call, taking your eyes off the road for even a *few seconds* can be the difference between a safe trip and a life-changing accident. Missouri law recognises the risks posed by distracted driving, which is why strict regulations are in place to limit *cell phone use* while operating a vehicle. Understanding these laws is not just important for passing your driving test—it is crucial for keeping yourself and everyone else on the road safe.

Missouri prohibits *all drivers under the age of 21* from using a *handheld electronic device* while driving. If you are a young driver, this means that you are not allowed to text, make calls, browse the internet, or engage in any other activity on your phone unless it is through a *hands-free* system. For *drivers over 21*, handheld cell phone use is still discouraged, and texting while driving is illegal for everyone, regardless of age. Law enforcement officers can stop and ticket you if they see you holding a phone, typing a message, or even appearing distracted by a mobile device while driving.

Texting while driving is particularly dangerous because it combines three types of distraction: *visual, manual, and cognitive*. When you read or send a text, your *eyes* leave the road, your *hands* leave the steering wheel, and your *mind* shifts away from the task of driving. Even if it only takes a few seconds, the distance you travel without full attention to the road can be significant. If you are driving at 55 mph, looking at your phone for *five seconds* is like driving the length of a football field with your eyes closed. In that short time, the car in front of you could slam on its brakes, a pedestrian could step into the street, or an animal could dart into your path—and you would not have enough time to react.

Missouri's *Siddens Bening Hands-Free Law*, which went into effect in 2023, applies to all drivers and makes it illegal to use a handheld device while operating a moving vehicle. You are allowed to use a *voice-activated or hands-free system*, such as Bluetooth, for phone calls, navigation, and other necessary functions. However, if you are holding your phone or using it manually while driving, you could be fined or face more serious penalties if your actions lead to an accident. First-time offenders may be fined up to *$150*, but repeat violations or texting while driving in a work or school zone can result in *higher fines, license points, or even suspension.*

While hands-free technology is permitted, it is important to remember that even using a *Bluetooth system* or a *speakerphone* can be distracting. You may not have to physically hold your phone, but talking to someone or focusing on a screen for directions can still pull your attention away from the road. This is why Missouri law encourages all drivers to minimise phone use altogether while driving. If you must make a call or check a message, the safest choice is to pull over in a *legal parking area* before reaching for your phone.

One of the biggest misconceptions about distracted driving is that experienced drivers can safely multitask behind the wheel. Many people believe that sending a quick text or glancing at their GPS is harmless, especially if they have been driving for years without an accident. However, research consistently shows that *no one*—regardless of skill or experience—is immune to the dangers of divided attention. Studies have found that drivers who use their phones while driving have reaction times comparable to those of *drunk drivers*. In both cases, delayed reactions and reduced awareness increase the risk of crashes, injuries, and fatalities.

The impact of cell phone use while driving extends beyond just individual drivers. Missouri's roadways are shared by *other vehicles, cyclists, pedestrians, and motorcyclists*, all of whom rely on drivers to stay alert and responsible. When you are distracted by your phone, you may fail to notice a *stop sign*, miss a *red light*, drift into another lane, or not see a pedestrian crossing the street. Accidents caused by distracted driving are not only preventable but often result in tragic consequences. Many fatal crashes involving cell phone use happen because drivers assumed they had everything under control—until it was too late.

Young drivers are particularly vulnerable to the dangers of distracted driving. Because newly licensed drivers are still developing *reaction skills and hazard awareness*, adding a cell phone into the mix increases the chances of making a mistake. Studies show that *teen drivers* are more likely than adults to use their phones while driving, even though they are the least experienced group on the road. This is why Missouri has strict rules for drivers under 21, enforcing *zero tolerance* for handheld phone use to protect young drivers from unnecessary risks.

To further combat the dangers of distracted driving, Missouri law enforcement conducts *high-visibility patrols and campaigns* to catch drivers who are using their phones behind the wheel. Officers may observe drivers at intersections, on highways, and in areas where distracted driving accidents are most common. If you are caught texting or using your phone illegally, you could receive a ticket, points on your driving record, and increased insurance rates. If your distracted driving leads to an accident that causes *injuries or fatalities*, the penalties become even more severe, with potential *criminal charges, large fines, and jail time.*

The simplest way to avoid the dangers of cell phone use while driving is to make a commitment to *stay focused on the road.* If you use your phone for navigation, set your destination before you start driving so you are not tempted to adjust it while moving. If you need to send a message or make a call, wait until you reach your destination or pull over safely. Many modern vehicles come with *built-in hands-free technology* to help reduce the need for handheld phone use, but even with these tools, it is best to limit distractions as much as possible.

Choosing to drive without distractions does not just help you avoid a ticket—it can save lives. Every time you get behind the wheel, you have a responsibility to yourself, your passengers, and everyone else on the road. A single moment of distraction is all it takes for a routine drive to turn into a disaster. By keeping your phone out of reach and focusing on driving, you are taking a simple yet powerful step toward making Missouri's roads safer for everyone.

The Missouri Drivers Permit Study Book 2025

CHAPTER 3
ROAD SIGNS AND TRAFFIC SIGNALS

3.1 REGULATORY SIGNS AND THEIR MEANINGS

Sign Type	Sign Name	Physical Description	What It Means	What to Do When You See the Sign
Stop Sign	Stop	An *octagonal* shape with a bright *red* background and *white* text that reads "STOP".	A *stop sign* requires that you come to a complete stop at the intersection, regardless of whether you see other vehicles or pedestrians.	You must bring your vehicle to a *complete stop* before the stop line, crosswalk, or intersection. Look both ways and proceed only when it's safe to do so.
Yield Sign	Yield	A *triangular* sign with a white background and a red border. The word *YIELD* is written in bold, *black* letters.	This sign tells you to *yield the right-of-way* to other vehicles or pedestrians. You should slow down and be prepared to stop.	Slow down or stop completely if necessary, and yield to other traffic or pedestrians. Proceed when it's safe.
Speed Limit Sign	Speed Limit	A rectangular sign with a white background and black text indicating a specific speed limit. There may be additional signs indicating conditions	This sign shows the maximum speed at which you can drive under ideal conditions. The speed limit can vary depending on the type of	Always drive within the posted speed limit. If the road conditions are poor (rain, snow, etc.), reduce your speed even if the limit

			that affect the limit.	road, area, or conditions.	remains the same.
School Zone Sign	School Zone		A rectangular sign with a *yellow* or *green* background and the words "SCHOOL ZONE" or an image of children walking. Often combined with a flashing light.	This sign indicates that you are entering an area near a school where children may be present. The speed limit in these areas is often reduced during school hours.	Slow down when entering a school zone and obey the posted speed limit, which is usually lower than on regular streets. Watch for children crossing.
Work Zone Sign	Construction Zone		A rectangular sign with an *orange* background and black text. It may include symbols such as a *worker with a shovel* or a *truck* icon.	This sign marks a construction zone where roadwork is taking place. The speed limit is usually reduced in these areas to protect workers and prevent accidents.	Slow down when you see this sign. Follow any posted signs with specific speed limits for the construction zone and watch for workers.
One-Way Sign	One-Way		A rectangular sign with a white background, and a black arrow indicating the direction of travel.	This sign indicates that traffic on this road must move in the direction shown by the arrow.	Only drive in the direction indicated by the sign. Never drive against the flow of traffic on a one-way street.
No Parking Sign	No Parking		A circular sign with a red border and a slashed "P" in	This sign indicates areas where parking is	Do not park in areas marked with this sign. Parking here

		the center, often with additional text explaining the restriction.	prohibited, often for safety, visibility, or to maintain traffic flow.	can result in fines or your vehicle being towed.
Maximum Speed Limit Sign	Maximum Speed Limit	A rectangular sign with black text showing the *maximum* allowed speed for a specific stretch of road. Often found on highways or roads where higher speeds are allowed.	This sign shows the highest legal speed you can drive under normal conditions. It is important to remember that the maximum speed is not always the safest.	Follow the posted maximum speed but always adjust based on weather, traffic, and road conditions.
Minimum Speed Limit Sign	Minimum Speed Limit	A rectangular sign with black text indicating the *minimum* speed allowed on highways or busy roads.	This sign indicates the lowest speed you can drive legally. Driving slower than the minimum speed can cause traffic congestion or accidents.	Make sure you maintain a speed that is at or above the posted minimum. If conditions allow, try to keep pace with the traffic flow.
No U-Turn Sign	No U-Turn	A circular sign with a black arrow making a U-turn and a red slash through it.	This sign indicates that making a U-turn at this intersection or on this road is prohibited.	Do not make a U-turn at this intersection. Look for alternate routes if you need to turn around.
Do Not Enter Sign	Do Not Enter	A circular red sign with a white	This sign means that vehicles are prohibited from entering	If you see this sign, turn around and find another way to reach

| | | horizontal bar in the center. | this roadway. It often appears at exit ramps or on one-way streets. | your destination. Entering here can lead to accidents or fines. |

Understanding the Importance of Regulatory Signs

Regulatory signs serve as critical components in the *safety* and *functionality* of the road system. They are designed to control the flow of traffic, ensure everyone follows the same rules, and prevent accidents. The physical appearance of each sign is carefully selected to catch the driver's attention, with distinct shapes and colors designed to convey urgency and clarity.

For example, the **stop sign** uses a red octagonal shape because red is universally associated with warning and urgency. The **yield sign**, with its triangle shape and red border, clearly conveys a need to slow down or stop, with the triangular shape suggesting a priority action. Similarly, the **speed limit signs** use black text on a white background to ensure visibility and readability from a distance, and their numbers indicate how fast you can legally travel.

While these signs are quite simple in their design, they carry significant legal weight. Failing to adhere to regulatory signs can lead to serious consequences, including fines, points on your driving record, or even the suspension of your driver's license. Understanding and following these signs is not only essential to passing your permit test but also to becoming a responsible driver.

By recognizing and following regulatory signs, you demonstrate your understanding of how traffic works and your commitment to safety. Properly obeying the rules of the road helps everyone, not just you, to get to their destination in one piece. Each regulatory sign, whether it's telling you to stop, yield, or maintain a specific speed, plays an important role in making sure that the roads are safe, predictable, and efficient.

In Missouri, as you study for your learner's permit, it's vital to familiarize yourself with all of these regulatory signs, paying attention to their shapes, colors, and meanings. Whether you are driving on the busy streets of Boston or the scenic highways in the western part of the state, you will encounter these signs regularly. Recognizing them quickly and responding appropriately is key to keeping yourself and others safe while driving.

The more you practice observing these signs, the more instinctive your reactions will become. Keep in mind that the *road* is shared by many other drivers, cyclists, and pedestrians, and following regulatory signs helps ensure smooth and safe interactions with everyone around you. Whether you're approaching an intersection, entering a school zone, or driving through construction, these signs help guide your actions and make you a more confident and capable driver.

3.2 WARNING SIGNS: WHAT TO WATCH OUT FOR

Warning signs are crucial for ensuring that you drive safely and are aware of potential hazards on the road ahead. These signs exist to alert you to changes in the driving environment that may require you to slow down, adjust your driving habits, or take extra caution. By learning to recognize these warning signs, you can anticipate road conditions and navigate more safely through different driving situations. Understanding what to look for and knowing how to respond when you see a warning sign is key to becoming a responsible, attentive driver.

In Missouri, warning signs are designed with specific shapes, colours, and symbols to make them easy to spot and understand. They are typically yellow or orange, often with black symbols or text, and they serve as a proactive way of preparing you for what lies ahead. Below, we will explore the most common warning signs you may encounter, detailing their appearance, meaning, and the proper actions you should take when you see them.

Warning Signs: What to Watch Out For

Sign Type	Sign Name	Physical Description	What It Means	What to Do When You See the Sign
Curve Sign	Right/Left Turn Ahead	A *yellow* diamond-shaped sign with an *arrow* indicating the direction of the turn.	This sign indicates a sharp curve in the road ahead, requiring drivers to slow down and navigate carefully.	Reduce your speed before entering the curve. Keep both hands on the wheel and ensure you maintain control of the vehicle while navigating the curve.
Slippery Road Sign	Slippery When Wet	A *yellow* diamond-shaped sign with a symbol of a car sliding on a slippery surface.	This sign warns that the road may be slippery when wet, making it easier for vehicles to lose traction.	Slow down when you see this sign, especially in wet weather. Avoid sudden braking or sharp turns. Increase following distance and stay alert for slippery conditions.

Pedestrian Crossing	Pedestrian Crossing	A *yellow* or *green* rectangular sign with an image of a walking person, often with flashing lights.	The sign alerts you to the possibility of pedestrians crossing the road ahead.	Slow down as you approach the crossing, and always be ready to stop for pedestrians. Yield to pedestrians waiting to cross or crossing the street.
Intersection Sign	Intersection Ahead	A *yellow* diamond-shaped sign with a symbol indicating an intersection ahead.	This sign signals that a junction with another road is approaching, and you should be prepared to yield or stop.	Slow down and be prepared to stop or yield depending on the situation. Always check for other vehicles and pedestrians before proceeding.
Deer Crossing Sign	Deer Crossing	A *yellow* diamond-shaped sign with the image of a deer.	This sign indicates that deer are known to cross the road in this area, especially at dawn and dusk.	Be extra vigilant when driving through wooded areas, particularly during early morning or evening. Slow down and keep an eye out for animals.
Lane Merge Sign	Lane Merge Ahead	A *yellow* diamond-shaped sign with arrows indicating merging lanes.	This sign warns that lanes will be merging, often from the right, and you should be prepared to	Yield to traffic in the lane you are merging into. Adjust your speed to match the

			adjust your speed or position.	flow of traffic and ensure it's safe before changing lanes.
Road Work Ahead Sign	Road Work Ahead	A *bright orange* diamond-shaped sign with a black symbol of a worker with a shovel.	This sign indicates that there is construction work or maintenance happening ahead, which may require lane changes or slowdowns.	Slow down and follow any additional signs or flaggers. Be prepared to stop or take a detour, and stay alert for workers or equipment.
Bump Sign	Bump Ahead	A *yellow* diamond-shaped sign with a symbol of a bump or raised surface.	This sign warns of a bump or sudden rise in the road surface, which could be uncomfortable for your vehicle.	Slow down as you approach the bump to avoid damaging your vehicle and ensure a smooth ride over the bump. Be cautious of any other hazards near the bump.
Winding Road Sign	Winding Road Ahead	A *yellow* diamond-shaped sign with a series of curving arrows.	This sign indicates that the road will wind or curve frequently, and you need to reduce your speed and stay alert.	Slow down and maintain a steady speed. Focus on navigating the turns and keep both hands on the wheel.
Stop Ahead Sign	Stop Sign Ahead	A *yellow* diamond-shaped sign with the word	This sign warns that a stop sign is ahead, and you will need to stop your	Begin slowing down and prepare to come to a complete stop when you

The Missouri Drivers Permit Study Book 2025

		"STOP" written on it.	vehicle completely at the intersection.	reach the intersection. Look both ways before proceeding.
Sharp Turn Ahead Sign	Sharp Turn Ahead	A *yellow* diamond-shaped sign with an arrow indicating a sharp turn.	This sign warns you of a sharp, sharp turn ahead, which requires you to slow down significantly.	Reduce your speed well before the turn to avoid losing control. Maintain control of the wheel and avoid sharp turns or sudden accelerations.
Railroad Crossing Sign	Railroad Crossing	A *yellow* diamond-shaped sign with a black railroad crossing symbol.	This sign warns of an upcoming railroad crossing where trains may pass through.	Slow down and look both ways for any oncoming trains. If lights are flashing, stop. Never try to drive across a railroad crossing when the gates are down.
End of Road Work Sign	End of Road Work	A *green* or *black* rectangular sign indicating the end of a construction zone.	This sign tells you that the construction zone is over and normal traffic conditions resume.	Return to the regular speed limit and proceed with caution as the road may still have some temporary issues such as uneven surfaces.
Steep Hill Sign	Steep Hill Downward	A *yellow* diamond-shaped sign with an	This sign indicates a steep decline ahead, which	Reduce your speed and shift to a lower gear to

		image of a car going downhill.	can make controlling your vehicle more difficult.	help control your speed when going down the hill. Stay in your lane and be cautious of other vehicles.
Crosswalk Sign	Crosswalk Ahead	A *yellow* or *green* rectangular sign with an image of a pedestrian walking, often with flashing lights.	This sign warns you of an upcoming crosswalk where pedestrians may be present.	Slow down and yield to pedestrians crossing the street. Always stop if someone is waiting to cross.
Sharp Curve Right/Left Sign	Sharp Curve Ahead (Right or Left)	A *yellow* diamond-shaped sign with an arrow indicating a sharp curve either to the right or left.	This sign warns of an upcoming sharp turn in the road, either to the left or right.	Slow down significantly, keep both hands on the wheel, and navigate the curve safely. Always check your surroundings before entering the curve.

How to Respond to Warning Signs

Warning signs are there to keep you informed about what lies ahead, and how you respond to them is key to maintaining safety on the road. While these signs may not always indicate an immediate hazard, they provide critical information to help you adjust your driving in advance.

For example, when you see the *slippery road* sign, it's a reminder that conditions may make it harder for your vehicle to maintain traction. Whether it's rain, snow, or ice, you should automatically begin to slow down and increase your following distance. Similarly, if you approach a *pedestrian crossing* sign, you should always be prepared to stop for any pedestrians who may be crossing the road. This not only helps keep you safe but also shows consideration for those walking along the streets.

The Missouri Drivers Permit Study Book 2025

Always remember that warning signs are not commands like regulatory signs (such as stop signs). They are there to give you a heads-up and allow you to adjust your driving habits accordingly. Being prepared and responsive will help you stay safe while driving in Missouri and anywhere else.

Knowing these warning signs and the appropriate actions to take when you encounter them will improve your ability to drive safely and confidently. They are an essential part of the driving experience, and understanding them thoroughly is crucial to passing your permit test and becoming a skilled driver. Always keep your eyes open for these signs and follow the advice they offer.

3.3 GUIDE SIGNS AND INFORMATION FOR DRIVERS

Guide signs and informational signs are a crucial part of the road system in Missouri. These signs help you navigate the streets, highways, and other roads by providing direction, giving you important information, and ensuring that you are aware of any services or facilities nearby. While regulatory signs are all about rules and warning signs are about potential hazards, guide and informational signs help you get from point A to point B safely and with ease.

Missouri, like most other states, uses a variety of guide signs to make driving easier and more predictable. Understanding the purpose of these signs, how to read them, and what actions you need to take when you see them will not only help you pass your permit test, but also make you a more confident and capable driver.

Below is a comprehensive catalogue of the most commonly encountered guide and informational signs that you will need to know for your Missouri driver's permit test in 2025.

Guide Signs and Information for Drivers

Sign Type	Sign Name	Physical Description	What It Means	What to Do When You See the Sign
Direction Sign	Exit Sign	A rectangular sign with a green background and white text, usually indicating exit numbers and the direction of travel.	This sign shows you the exit from the highway or road you're traveling on, guiding you to your desired destination.	Follow the exit sign and move to the appropriate lane ahead of time. Ensure you signal to other drivers and slow down as necessary when taking the exit.

The Missouri Drivers Permit Study Book 2025

Route Sign	Route Marker	A rectangular sign with a white background and black text or number indicating a highway or route.	This sign tells you the number of the highway or route you're traveling on. It helps you navigate the highway system.	Make sure you are on the correct route by confirming with your GPS or a map. Follow the sign until you reach your desired exit or destination.
Mileage Sign	Mileage Marker	A green sign with white text indicating the number of miles to a destination, town, or city.	This sign tells you how far you are from a particular location. It's used to help you track your progress on the road.	Use the mileage marker to help gauge how much farther you need to travel. It can be especially useful when traveling on highways to check how much longer your trip will be.
Intersection Sign	Crossroad Intersection	A rectangular sign with a black symbol of a perpendicular road crossing your current road.	This sign warns that an intersection is ahead where another road crosses your current road.	Slow down and be prepared to stop or yield at the intersection. Check for vehicles or pedestrians before proceeding.
Speed Limit Sign	Speed Limit	A rectangular sign with a white background and black text indicating the maximum or	This sign tells you the maximum or minimum speed you can legally drive at on a specific	Always adhere to the speed limit indicated, but be mindful of road conditions. Adjust your speed

			minimum speed allowed.	section of the road.	accordingly if weather or traffic conditions require it.
Service Signs	Gas, Rest Area, Food		A rectangular sign with symbols and/or text indicating services like gas stations, rest areas, or food. These signs typically have a blue background with white text or symbols.	These signs indicate the location of essential services like gas stations, rest stops, or food, helping you plan your breaks or fuel stops.	Use these signs to plan stops for fuel, food, or rest. Follow the sign and be mindful of the distance to the service area to ensure you don't run low on fuel.
Road Name Sign	Street Name Sign		A rectangular sign with a white background and black text showing the name of the street or road.	This sign shows you the name of the street or road you're on, helping you to orient yourself and find your way around.	Pay attention to street names when navigating through unfamiliar areas. Use them to confirm your location or when following directions.
Toll Road Sign	Toll Booth		A rectangular or square sign, often with a black image of a toll booth or a dollar sign. It indicates that the road ahead has tolls.	This sign tells you that you will need to pay a toll to continue on the road.	Prepare to stop at a toll booth and pay the required fee. Some tolls may have electronic payment systems, so ensure you have the proper

The Missouri Drivers Permit Study Book 2025

				payment method ready.
Hospital Sign	Hospital Ahead	A rectangular sign with a white background and a symbol of a hospital, indicating the direction and distance to the nearest hospital.	This sign provides directions to the nearest hospital, which can be helpful in emergency situations.	Follow the sign to the hospital if you are in need of medical assistance or if you're helping someone who requires urgent care.
Parking Sign	Public Parking	A rectangular sign with a blue background and a white "P" symbol, indicating the location of public parking.	This sign helps you locate designated parking areas for public use.	Follow the sign to find a parking area, but make sure to check any time restrictions or fees before parking.
Exit Ramp Sign	Off-Ramp Exit	A rectangular sign with a green background and white text, indicating which ramp leads to an exit and the direction of travel.	This sign shows you the off-ramp you need to take to leave the highway or interstate.	Prepare to move into the correct lane and follow the exit ramp. Slow down to match the exit's speed requirements, and signal appropriately.
Truck Route Sign	Truck Route	A rectangular sign with a black truck symbol and text indicating a route designated for trucks.	This sign designates specific routes for trucks to ensure they travel on safer, more suitable roads.	If you're driving a truck or large vehicle, follow this sign to ensure you're on the correct route. Drivers of smaller vehicles should be

					aware and avoid these routes if possible.
Exit Ramp Distance Sign	Exit Distance	A rectangular sign with a green background and white text indicating the distance to the next exit ramp.	This sign tells you how far away the next exit ramp is, so you can prepare in advance.		Check the sign and prepare to take the exit in the indicated distance. Move to the correct lane ahead of time to avoid last-minute lane changes.
Rest Area Sign	Rest Area Ahead	A rectangular sign with a blue background and a white symbol of a bed or rest area.	This sign indicates that a rest area is ahead, where you can stop and take a break from driving.		If you're feeling tired or need a break, follow this sign to a rest area where you can stop safely and refresh yourself.
Route Number Sign	Interstate Route	A rectangular sign with a blue shield or circle, featuring a number in the center. It indicates the route number of the interstate or highway.	This sign shows the specific number of the interstate or highway you are driving on, helping you navigate through long trips.		Ensure you are on the correct interstate or highway. Follow the route number signs to stay on track for your destination.
Bike Route Sign	Bike Route	A rectangular sign with a green background and a white bicycle symbol, indicating a	This sign marks routes specifically designated for cyclists.		If you're cycling, follow these signs to stay on designated bike paths. Drivers should be aware of

| | | bike-friendly route. | | cyclists when they see these signs. |

Understanding Guide and Informational Signs

Guide signs play a pivotal role in making your journey smoother and safer. They provide the necessary information you need to make informed decisions while on the road. Whether you are trying to navigate unfamiliar areas or just need to find a place to stop for a break, guide and informational signs are designed to help you make the right choices.

The majority of these signs are color-coded and follow specific shapes to make them easily identifiable. For example, *green* guide signs typically indicate directional information, such as highway exits or mile markers. *Blue* signs generally point to services such as food, rest areas, and medical facilities. *Brown* signs often provide information about recreational areas, such as national parks or beaches, giving you insight into points of interest nearby.

As a new driver in Missouri, paying attention to these signs can help you better navigate the road and avoid unnecessary confusion or stress. They are also crucial for preventing accidents, as they provide you with the opportunity to make decisions in advance rather than react hastily when you find yourself in an unfamiliar or dangerous situation.

For example, seeing a *mileage marker* sign on a long stretch of highway helps you track your progress and estimate how much farther you need to go. Similarly, when you see a *hospital ahead* sign, you'll know exactly where to head if you or someone else is in need of medical attention.

In addition to their practical applications, these signs are also vital in maintaining efficient traffic flow. By following guide signs, you ensure that you're on the correct path, which minimizes congestion and confusion for everyone on the road.

By studying and understanding guide signs, you are equipping yourself with the tools needed to drive confidently and responsibly. The more familiar you are with these signs, the easier it will be to navigate Missouri and other areas without stress or confusion. Always be mindful of what each sign tells you, and be sure to take the proper actions to keep your journey safe and efficient. With this knowledge, you'll be one step closer to mastering the art of safe and responsible driving.

3.4 TRAFFIC SIGNALS AND PAVEMENT MARKINGS

Traffic signals and pavement markings control how you navigate intersections, lanes, and roadways, ensuring safety and order for everyone on the road. Each signal and marking carries a specific meaning, guiding you on when to stop, go, yield, or change lanes. Some signals are universal, while others may be unique to certain locations. Similarly, pavement markings serve as visual cues, often working alongside signs and signals to give you extra guidance about lane usage, passing zones, pedestrian crossings, and road boundaries. Understanding these symbols thoroughly will not only help you pass your permit test but will also make you a more confident and responsible driver.

Traffic signals are electronic lights positioned at intersections, pedestrian crossings, and other critical points on the road. They are designed to manage traffic movement by using a standardised colour system that tells you when to *stop, proceed, or slow down*. Some traffic signals also include arrows, flashing lights, or special signs to provide additional instructions.

Pavement markings, on the other hand, are painted lines, arrows, and symbols on the road surface. These markings define lanes, indicate stopping points, highlight crosswalks, and warn of specific driving conditions. They are often colour-coded, with *white* and *yellow* being the most common. While signs and signals give explicit commands, pavement markings reinforce and clarify these rules, ensuring drivers follow proper lane discipline and right-of-way rules.

The table below provides a comprehensive breakdown of Missouri's traffic signals and pavement markings, giving you detailed descriptions of what they look like, what they mean, and how you should respond when you see them.

Traffic Signals and Their Meanings

Traffic Signal	Physical Description	What It Means	What to Do When You See It
Red Light	Circular red light, typically at the top of a traffic signal	*Stop completely.* You cannot proceed until the light changes.	Come to a full stop before the intersection or crosswalk. Wait for a green light before continuing.
Yellow Light	Circular yellow light, usually in the middle of a traffic signal	*Warning that the light is about to turn red.*	Slow down and prepare to stop. If you are too close to stop safely, proceed cautiously.
Green Light	Circular green light, typically at the bottom of a traffic signal	*Go if it is safe to do so.*	Proceed through the intersection if the way is clear. Watch for pedestrians and other vehicles.
Flashing Red Light	Red light that blinks continuously	*Same as a STOP sign.* You must stop and yield before proceeding.	Stop completely, check for other traffic, then proceed when it is safe.

Flashing Yellow Light	Yellow light that blinks continuously	*Caution—proceed with care.*	Slow down and be alert to cross traffic or hazards. Proceed carefully.
Red Arrow	Red arrow pointing left or right	*Do not turn in the direction of the arrow.*	Stay stopped until the light changes to a green arrow or a green light.
Yellow Arrow	Yellow arrow pointing left or right	*The turn signal is about to change to red.*	If you are already in the intersection, complete your turn quickly and safely. If not, prepare to stop.
Green Arrow	Green arrow pointing left or right	*You may turn in the direction of the arrow.*	Make your turn but yield to pedestrians and other vehicles with the right-of-way.
Pedestrian Signal - "WALK"	White symbol of a walking figure	*Pedestrians may cross the street.*	Allow pedestrians to cross before proceeding.
Pedestrian Signal - "DON'T WALK"	Orange hand symbol or text saying "DON'T WALK"	*Pedestrians must not begin crossing.*	If pedestrians are already in the crosswalk, let them finish crossing before you move.

Pavement Markings and Their Meanings

Pavement Marking	Physical Description	What It Means	What to Do When You See It
Solid White Line	Thick white line separating lanes in the same direction	*Lane changes are discouraged but not illegal.*	Stay in your lane unless absolutely necessary.
Broken White Line	Dotted white line separating lanes in the same direction	*You may change lanes if it is safe.*	Check your mirrors and blind spots before changing lanes.
Double Solid White Lines	Two thick white lines running parallel	*Lane changes are prohibited.*	Remain in your lane—do not cross these lines.

The Missouri Drivers Permit Study Book 2025

Solid Yellow Line	Thick yellow line separating lanes moving in opposite directions	*No passing allowed.*	Stay in your lane and do not attempt to pass another vehicle.
Broken Yellow Line	Dotted yellow line separating lanes moving in opposite directions	*Passing is allowed when safe.*	If the way is clear, you may pass another vehicle carefully.
Double Solid Yellow Lines	Two parallel yellow lines	*Passing is strictly prohibited.*	Remain in your lane. Do not cross unless turning into a driveway.
Yellow Line with Broken and Solid Sides	One side has a solid yellow line; the other has a broken line	*Passing is allowed only for vehicles on the broken side.*	If you are on the side with the broken line, you may pass when safe. If on the solid side, do not pass.
White Arrows on the Road	Painted arrows pointing straight, left, or right	*Indicate permitted movements for each lane.*	Follow the direction of the arrow to stay in compliance.
Crosswalk	White painted lines, often at intersections	*Indicates pedestrian crossing zones.*	Slow down and be prepared to stop for pedestrians.
Stop Line	Thick white line before a crosswalk or intersection	*Marks where vehicles must stop at stop signs or signals.*	Stop behind the line and wait for the appropriate signal.
Railroad Crossing Markings	White "X" and "RR" symbols painted on the pavement	*Indicates an upcoming railroad crossing.*	Slow down, look for trains, and stop if necessary.

Recognising and understanding these signals and markings will make you a safer, more responsible driver. Whether you are stopping at a red light, yielding to pedestrians at a crosswalk, or following lane restrictions, each signal and marking plays a role in keeping traffic flowing efficiently and preventing accidents. Missouri's roads are carefully designed to keep drivers, cyclists, and pedestrians safe, but that only works when everyone understands and follows the rules. When you drive, be sure to look ahead, stay aware of your surroundings, and respond correctly to every traffic signal and pavement marking you encounter.

CHAPTER 4
SAFE DRIVING PRACTICES

4.1 DEFENSIVE DRIVING TECHNIQUES

The ability to drive defensively is one of the most valuable skills you can develop as you prepare to take the road. In Missouri, where road conditions, traffic density, and unpredictable driver behaviours vary from city to rural highway, knowing how to anticipate and respond to hazards can mean the difference between a safe trip and a collision. Defensive driving is not about assuming every driver around you is reckless, but rather about staying *proactive, alert, and prepared* for any situation that may arise. It is a mindset and a method of driving that protects you, your passengers, and others on the road by reducing risks before they turn into real dangers.

One of the core principles of defensive driving is *situational awareness*. This means constantly monitoring your surroundings, checking your mirrors frequently, and staying alert to vehicles ahead, behind, and beside you. Unlike passive drivers who only focus on what is directly in front of them, a defensive driver scans the entire road environment. You should always be looking ahead, anticipating potential problems before they happen. For example, if you see brake lights flashing several cars ahead, you should be prepared to slow down even before the vehicle directly in front of you reacts. If a car is weaving in and out of traffic aggressively, it is best to assume that driver may not be paying full attention—give them extra space so you are not caught off guard if they make a sudden move.

Maintaining a *safe following distance* is another critical defensive driving technique. Missouri's roads have varying speed limits, and in higher-speed areas such as highways, stopping distances increase significantly. The *three-second rule* is a widely recommended technique to ensure you have enough space between your vehicle and the one in front of you. To use it, pick a fixed point on the road, such as a sign or a tree. When the vehicle ahead passes that point, start counting: "one thousand one, one thousand two, one thousand three." If you reach the same point before finishing the count, you are too close and should slow down to create more distance. This rule should be extended to *six seconds or more* in poor weather conditions, such as heavy rain, fog, or snow, which are all common in Missouri during different seasons. Wet roads reduce tire traction, and icy patches can be almost invisible, making increased stopping distance crucial.

Understanding *right-of-way rules* and anticipating how other drivers might react is another essential aspect of defensive driving. Even if you legally have the right-of-way at an intersection, you must be prepared for the possibility that another driver may ignore or misunderstand the rules. Many crashes occur because one driver assumes another will yield when they do not. A defensive driver always waits for confirmation before proceeding—whether it is through eye contact, a wave, or the movement of the other vehicle. When approaching an intersection, especially one without traffic signals, you should reduce your speed slightly and be prepared to stop if necessary. Always check cross-traffic twice before moving forward, even if you have a green light, to ensure that no one is running the signal.

Another key strategy is *identifying escape routes*. This means always being aware of an alternate path you can take if the unexpected happens. For example, if a car suddenly slams on its brakes in front of you, knowing whether you have an open lane to swerve into—or whether a shoulder is available—can make all the difference. If you find yourself boxed in with no escape route, it is crucial to start slowing down early to prevent a rear-end collision. When driving on Missouri highways, where large trucks frequently travel alongside smaller vehicles, always be mindful of their blind spots. Trucks take much longer to stop, and their drivers have limited visibility. If you need to pass a truck, do so quickly but safely, and never linger beside it in a blind zone.

Being prepared for *hazardous weather conditions* is especially important in Missouri, where sudden thunderstorms, high winds, and icy conditions can drastically change driving conditions. A defensive driver does not just react to the weather but *adapts in advance*. If rain begins to fall, turning your headlights on immediately not only helps you see better but also makes you more visible to others. In fog, using low-beam headlights instead of high beams prevents glare from reflecting off the mist and impairing your vision. When roads are icy, braking should be done *gently and gradually*, as sudden braking can cause your vehicle to slide. Steering smoothly and avoiding sudden acceleration or lane changes will help you maintain control. If you ever find yourself in a skid, remember to *steer into the skid*—this means turning your wheel in the direction the back of your car is sliding to regain control.

Defensive driving also includes managing *distractions* inside your own vehicle. Modern cars come with various technological conveniences, such as touch-screen controls, GPS navigation, and Bluetooth connectivity, but these can quickly become sources of distraction if not handled properly. The best practice is to set up all controls—such as adjusting mirrors, inputting GPS destinations, and selecting music—*before* you start driving. If you need to make adjustments while driving, pull over safely rather than taking your hands off the wheel or your eyes off the road. Even a momentary distraction, such as checking a notification on your phone, can have deadly consequences. At 60 mph, looking at your phone for just three seconds means your car will travel about *the length of a football field* completely unsupervised. Defensive drivers understand that no message, call, or adjustment is worth the risk.

Managing *road rage situations* is another key defensive driving skill. It is not enough to just drive carefully—you must also know how to respond when others do not. Missouri has its fair share of aggressive drivers who tailgate, honk excessively, or make rude gestures. If you encounter someone behaving aggressively on the road, the best approach is to *avoid engaging*. Do not make eye contact, do not retaliate with gestures or honks, and most importantly, do not speed up or brake-check them in response. If a driver is following too closely, signal early when turning or changing lanes to give them plenty of notice. If someone is acting especially dangerous, such as swerving at you or trying to force you off the road, call 911 or drive to a public place like a police station or well-lit parking lot rather than going home.

Knowing how to *react in emergencies* is another part of defensive driving. Tire blowouts, brake failures, and engine stalls can happen unexpectedly. If you experience a tire blowout, *grip the steering wheel firmly* and avoid slamming the brakes—gradually ease off the accelerator and let your vehicle slow down while steering straight. If your brakes fail, rapidly *pump the brake pedal* to try and restore pressure, shift into a lower gear to slow the car, and use the emergency brake as a last resort. If your engine stalls on a highway, signal immediately and try to coast to the right shoulder. Keep your hazard lights on and stay inside your car unless it is unsafe to do so.

At night, defensive driving becomes even more important. Reduced visibility means you must rely on headlights, reflections, and your awareness of other vehicles' lights to navigate safely. Always *dim your high beams* when approaching another vehicle to avoid blinding the other driver. If a driver behind you refuses to lower their high beams, use the rearview mirror's night mode or adjust it slightly to deflect the glare. Watch out for animals crossing rural roads at night—Missouri has a high population of deer, which are especially active at dusk and dawn. If you see one deer, assume there may be more, and reduce your speed rather than trying to swerve.

The best defensive drivers are *predictable and cautious*, but not overly timid. Hesitation at the wrong moment—such as stopping suddenly when it is unnecessary—can confuse other drivers and lead to rear-end collisions. A confident driver communicates clearly through proper use of turn signals, brake lights, and hand gestures when needed. You should always assume that not everyone on the road is as careful as you, and drive accordingly. By mastering defensive driving techniques, you not only increase your chances of passing your permit test with ease, but you also develop the habits that will keep you safe every time you get behind the wheel.

4.2 SHARING THE ROAD WITH PEDESTRIANS AND CYCLISTS

The ability to safely share the road with *pedestrians* and *cyclists* is just as important as knowing how to navigate traffic. Unlike motor vehicles, pedestrians and cyclists do not have the same level of protection in the event of a crash, which means that even a minor mistake on your part could have devastating consequences for them. Understanding right-of-way laws, recognising high-risk areas, and practicing caution whenever people on foot or bicycles are nearby will not only keep everyone safer but will also help you develop the responsible driving habits that Missouri law expects from every motorist.

Pedestrians are the most vulnerable road users, and Missouri's traffic laws give them specific protections to ensure their safety. The most fundamental rule you must remember is that *pedestrians always have the right-of-way in crosswalks*. Whether the crosswalk is marked with painted lines or unmarked at an intersection, you are required to yield whenever a pedestrian is crossing. The law does not make exceptions for whether they are walking slowly, distracted, or crossing at an inconvenient time—you must stop and allow them to cross fully before proceeding. If a pedestrian is stepping off the curb and into a marked crosswalk, you need to stop well before the crosswalk line, as stopping too close can pressure them to hurry or make it harder for other drivers to see them. If there is a pedestrian island in the middle of a divided road, you must wait until they reach the island before proceeding if they started crossing on your side.

Even in places where no marked crosswalks exist, Missouri law expects you to use *reasonable caution* when pedestrians are present. In neighbourhoods, shopping centres, or downtown areas where people commonly cross outside of designated spots, you should always reduce your speed and be ready to stop. Jaywalking—crossing the street outside of a crosswalk—is common, and while it is technically against the law for pedestrians, that does not mean you are allowed to ignore them or proceed as if they are not there. The law expects you to yield whenever necessary to avoid a collision. You should also be aware that children and elderly pedestrians may not react as quickly as other people. A child playing near the street may suddenly run into traffic without looking, and older pedestrians may walk more slowly or have difficulty judging the speed of oncoming cars. These are situations where you need to drive with heightened awareness and expect the unexpected.

One of the most dangerous mistakes drivers make is *passing vehicles that are stopped at a crosswalk*. If you are approaching a multi-lane road and see a vehicle in another lane stopping near a crosswalk, you should never assume they are stopping for no reason. It is very likely that a pedestrian is crossing, but your view is blocked by the stopped vehicle. Missouri law requires you to stop as well, even if you do not immediately see a pedestrian, because proceeding forward could result in striking someone who is walking in front of the stopped vehicle. Always wait until you have a clear view of the entire crosswalk before continuing.

School zones and areas near parks require extra caution because children are often present. Missouri has specific speed limits in school zones, usually reduced to *25 mph or lower* during school hours. Flashing yellow lights or posted signs will indicate when these reduced speed limits are in effect, and you are expected to obey them regardless of whether you see children nearby. School zones often have crossing guards directing pedestrian traffic, and their instructions *must* be followed just as you would obey a traffic signal. Failing to yield to a crossing guard's instructions can result in serious penalties and endanger lives.

Another area where you must be extra cautious is near public transit stops. Missouri has multiple transit systems, including MetroLink and local bus services, which frequently stop to pick up and drop off passengers. If a bus is pulled over at a bus stop, it is highly likely that people will be stepping off and crossing the road. Always slow down when passing a stopped bus and check for pedestrians who may suddenly step into your path.

Cyclists, like pedestrians, are also vulnerable road users, but they have a unique set of rules that you need to be aware of when sharing the road with them. In Missouri, cyclists are legally considered *vehicles*, which means they have the same rights and responsibilities as cars. This includes obeying traffic signals, stop signs, and lane markings. However, due to their smaller size and slower speed, they require extra care from drivers to ensure their safety.

One of the most critical rules when driving near cyclists is maintaining a *safe passing distance*. Missouri law requires that you leave at least *three feet of space* between your vehicle and a cyclist when passing them on the road. If a road is too narrow to allow this space, you must wait until it is safe to pass. Attempting to squeeze by too closely can cause the cyclist to lose balance or be forced off the road. If a cyclist is riding near the right edge of a lane and you are unsure whether you have enough space to pass safely, it is better to slow down and wait rather than risk a dangerous close pass. On roads with multiple lanes, you should move into the next lane over if possible when passing to give the cyclist extra room.

Cyclists are allowed to ride in the centre of a lane when necessary for their safety. This often happens when the road is too narrow for cars to pass safely within the same lane. If you encounter a cyclist riding in the middle of the lane, do not attempt to squeeze past them—wait until you have enough room to move into the next lane before passing. Many drivers mistakenly believe that cyclists are required to ride as far to the right as possible at all times, but Missouri law allows them to take the full lane when needed.

Intersections are especially dangerous for cyclists because many drivers fail to see them or misjudge their speed. One of the most common causes of cyclist injuries is the *right hook*—when a driver makes a right turn without noticing a cyclist traveling straight in the same direction. If you are making a right turn at an intersection or driveway, always check your *blind spot* to ensure no cyclists are coming up alongside you. A cyclist traveling at 15–20 mph can easily enter your blind spot if you do not check properly. Even if you have your turn signal on, a cyclist may assume you will wait for them to pass before turning. To avoid a right-hook collision, always slow down before turning and double-check for cyclists before crossing into their path.

Another common mistake drivers make is opening their car doors without checking for cyclists. This is known as *dooring*, and it happens when a driver or passenger opens a car door into the path of an oncoming cyclist. To prevent this, Missouri encourages drivers to use the *Dutch Reach* technique—opening the car door with the hand furthest from the door. This forces you to turn your body and naturally check for approaching cyclists before opening the door.

Cyclists often use *hand signals* to indicate turns or lane changes, just like how cars use turn signals. If a cyclist extends their left arm straight out, they are signaling a *left turn*. If they extend their right arm straight out, they are signaling a *right turn*. If they hold their left arm down at a 90-degree angle, they are indicating a *stop or slowing down*. Recognising these signals will help you anticipate their movements and avoid conflicts on the road.

Nighttime cycling presents additional risks, as cyclists are harder to see in low-light conditions. Missouri law requires cyclists riding after dark to have a *white front light* and a *red rear reflector* or light. As a driver, you should always be extra vigilant when driving at night, especially in areas without streetlights. Cyclists may not always have the best visibility gear, so scanning ahead and reducing your speed in dark areas will help prevent collisions.

The key to safely sharing the road with pedestrians and cyclists is *patience, awareness, and respect*. When you drive with the understanding that these road users are more exposed to harm, you naturally begin to make decisions that prioritise safety over convenience. A few extra seconds of caution at an intersection, a wider berth when passing, or a second glance in your mirror before opening your door can be the difference between a normal drive and a tragic accident. Developing these habits now will not only help you pass your permit test but will also make you a safer and more responsible driver every time you get behind the wheel.

4.3 ADJUSTING TO WEATHER AND ROAD CONDITIONS

Missouri's weather can be unpredictable, and road conditions change quickly depending on the season, time of day, and surrounding environment. One moment, the sky may be clear and the roads dry, and the next, a sudden downpour, patch of ice, or thick fog can turn driving into a real challenge. Knowing how to *adjust your driving to match the weather and road conditions* is not just about comfort—it is about safety. When conditions change, you must change the way you drive. If you do not, you are putting yourself and others at risk.

Rain is one of the most common weather conditions you will encounter in Missouri, and while it may not seem as dangerous as snow or ice, wet roads can be extremely slippery, especially when it first starts raining. Oil, dirt, and other debris on the road mix with water, creating a slick surface that reduces traction. This can lead to *hydroplaning*, where your tyres lose contact with the road and start gliding on a thin layer of water. If this happens, you will have little to no control over your vehicle. To reduce the risk of hydroplaning, you should always slow down when it starts raining, avoid sudden braking, and increase your following distance. Your *tyres* play a crucial role in maintaining grip on wet roads, so you should regularly check their tread depth. Missouri law requires at least *2/32 of an inch* of tread, but in rainy conditions, deeper tread provides better traction. Worn-out tyres increase your risk of skidding, especially when driving at higher speeds.

Heavy rain also reduces *visibility*, making it harder to see road markings, signs, and other vehicles. Missouri law requires you to *turn on your headlights whenever your windshield wipers are in use*, even during the daytime. This makes it easier for other drivers to see you. If the rain is so heavy that you can barely see the road ahead, the safest option is to pull over in a safe location, such as a parking lot or rest area, and wait for conditions to improve. If you must keep driving, reduce your speed significantly and follow the road's edge markings rather than trying to rely on blurry taillights ahead of you.

Fog is another weather condition that can appear unexpectedly, especially in the early morning or late at night. The biggest danger with fog is that it limits your ability to see ahead. Many drivers make the mistake of turning on their high beams in fog, but this actually *makes visibility worse* because the light reflects off the fog and creates glare. Instead, you should use *low beam headlights* or, if your vehicle has them, *fog lights*, which are designed to cut through the mist without reflecting back into your eyes. When driving in fog, you should also increase your following distance and avoid sudden lane changes. Even if you can see the road in front of you, other drivers may not see you until the last moment. Staying in your lane and keeping a steady speed will help prevent sudden surprises. If the fog becomes too thick to drive safely, you should pull off the road completely and turn on your hazard lights to alert other drivers.

Snow and ice are among the most dangerous conditions you will face, especially during Missouri's winter months. Ice can be invisible in certain conditions, forming what is known as *black ice*—a thin, transparent layer that blends with the road surface. Black ice is most common in the early morning and late evening, when temperatures are just below freezing. Bridges, overpasses, and shaded areas freeze first because they are exposed to cold air on multiple sides, so these areas can be icy even if the rest of the road appears clear. If you hit a patch of ice, you should *never* slam on the brakes, as this will cause your tyres to lock up and make you lose control. Instead, you should ease off the accelerator and steer *gently* in the direction you want to go.

Before driving in snowy or icy conditions, you should always *clear all snow and ice from your vehicle*, including your roof, hood, windows, and mirrors. If you leave snow on your roof, it can slide down and block your windshield when you brake. If your windows are foggy or covered in frost, take the time to let your defrosters clear them completely before driving. Many crashes in winter happen simply because drivers fail to clear their windows properly and cannot see their surroundings.

Speed control is critical when driving in snow or ice. The posted speed limit may be *too fast* for the conditions, and Missouri law states that you must adjust your speed to match the road conditions, even if that means driving significantly below the limit. You should *accelerate and brake slowly* to avoid skidding, and you should never use cruise control on slippery roads, as it can make your car accelerate when you least expect it. If your vehicle has *antilock brakes (ABS)*, you should apply firm, steady pressure to the brake pedal rather than pumping it. If your car starts to slide, *steer in the direction of the skid* to regain control.

Strong winds can also create challenges, especially on open highways, bridges, and rural roads where there are fewer windbreaks. Large vehicles like trucks, trailers, and buses are more affected by wind gusts, and they may swerve unexpectedly. If you are passing a large vehicle during high winds, you should *give extra space* and be prepared for a sudden shift in its position. Your own car may also be pushed sideways in a strong gust, so keeping a firm grip on the steering wheel and avoiding sudden movements is important.

Missouri is also known for severe weather, including *thunderstorms* and *tornadoes*. If you are caught in a thunderstorm while driving, you should reduce your speed and be cautious of *standing water* on the road, which can cause hydroplaning. If a tornado warning is issued and you see a tornado in the distance, *do not try to outrun it in your car*. Instead, look for a sturdy building to take shelter in. If no buildings are available, you should park your car, get out, and find a low-lying area like a ditch to lie in, covering your head with your hands. Overpasses are *not* safe places to take shelter, as winds can be even stronger underneath them.

At night, road conditions can be more difficult to judge, even when the weather is clear. *Glare from headlights* can make it hard to see, especially on wet or icy roads where light reflections are stronger. You should always *dim your high beams* when approaching another vehicle to avoid blinding other drivers. On unfamiliar roads, reducing your speed and scanning ahead for obstacles can help prevent sudden surprises.

Potholes and uneven road surfaces are common in Missouri, especially after winter when ice expands and cracks the pavement. Hitting a deep pothole at high speed can damage your tyres, suspension, or even your vehicle's frame. If you see a pothole ahead, you should slow down *before* reaching it rather than slamming on the brakes at the last second, as sudden braking can make the impact worse. If it is safe to do so, steering around a pothole is the best option. However, if traffic conditions prevent this, you should at least reduce your speed and drive over it as smoothly as possible.

Adjusting to different weather and road conditions requires constant awareness, patience, and the ability to *think ahead*. The best drivers are not just the ones who follow the rules when conditions are ideal but the ones who know how to adapt when things change. Developing the habit of slowing down, increasing your following distance, and staying alert to your surroundings will make you a safer driver in all conditions. Being prepared for the unexpected will not only help you pass your permit test but will also keep you and others safe on the road every time you drive.

4.4 MANAGING DRIVER FATIGUE AND DISTRACTIONS

Drowsy driving is just as dangerous as driving under the influence of alcohol. When you are *tired behind the wheel*, your reaction time slows, your ability to focus decreases, and your judgment becomes impaired. You may think you can push through exhaustion, but fatigue has a way of creeping up on you without warning. A moment of drowsiness is all it takes to drift into another lane, miss a stop sign, or fail to notice a car braking in front of you. Missouri's highways, rural roads, and even city streets can be treacherous if you are not fully alert. No matter how experienced you are, *fatigue can turn even the safest driver into a danger on the road.*

Long stretches of highway, especially in Missouri's more rural areas, can make drowsy driving even worse. The monotony of driving on open roads, particularly at night, can lull you into a state of *highway hypnosis*, where you become less aware of your surroundings and react more slowly to hazards. This is particularly common on roads like Interstate 70, which runs across the state and can feel endless when you are tired. If you catch yourself *blinking frequently, struggling to keep your head up, missing exits, or drifting slightly within your lane*, these are warning signs that you need to stop driving and rest.

The Missouri Drivers Permit Study Book 2025

You might think rolling down the windows, turning up the music, or sipping on coffee will keep you awake, but these methods only provide short bursts of alertness. The only real solution for *driver fatigue* is to get enough rest before you drive. If you are planning a long trip, you should make sure you get at least *seven to eight hours of sleep* the night before. If you feel sleepy while driving, the safest thing to do is pull over at a rest stop or safe location and take a short nap. Even a *20-minute nap* can make a significant difference in your alertness level. If you are on a longer trip, planning *breaks every two hours* can help keep your mind fresh and prevent fatigue from setting in.

Driving at night increases the risk of fatigue because your body's natural rhythm is telling you to sleep. Your eyes may struggle to adjust to the darkness, and the steady glow of headlights can make it harder to stay alert. If you must drive late at night, making sure you have rested beforehand and keeping your vehicle's interior dim (but not too dark) can help. You should also be aware of *shift workers* and truck drivers, who often drive through the night and may be experiencing fatigue themselves. Sharing the road with a tired driver is just as dangerous as being one. If you notice another vehicle *drifting between lanes, slowing down erratically, or reacting too late to traffic signals*, the driver may be struggling to stay awake. Giving extra space and being prepared for sudden movements can help you avoid an accident.

Distractions are another major threat to safe driving, and they come in many forms. You might picture *texting while driving* as the most obvious distraction—and it is one of the most dangerous—but anything that takes your focus off the road can be just as hazardous. Eating, adjusting the radio, talking to passengers, or even daydreaming can prevent you from noticing important details on the road. The moment your attention shifts, you put yourself at risk of making a critical mistake. Missouri's roads are filled with intersections, stop-and-go city traffic, and high-speed highway zones where distractions can have deadly consequences.

Missouri law prohibits *texting while driving for all drivers under the age of 21*, but even if you are older, using a phone behind the wheel is still incredibly risky. Reading or sending a text takes your eyes off the road for an average of *five seconds*. If you are driving at *55 mph*, that means you will travel the length of a football field without looking up. A lot can happen in that distance—cars can stop suddenly, pedestrians can step into the road, and hazards can appear out of nowhere. If you need to *send a message, answer a call, or check your GPS*, the safest option is to pull over and do it when you are stopped. Many modern vehicles have *hands-free features*, but even talking on a Bluetooth device can be distracting if your mind is not fully engaged with the road.

Passengers can also be a major source of distraction, especially if you are driving with friends. Conversations, laughter, and even arguments can pull your attention away from the task at hand. If someone in your car is being too distracting, you have the right to *ask them to quiet down or wait until you are parked*. It is your responsibility to maintain control of the vehicle, and that includes making sure your passengers are not interfering with your focus.

Eating and drinking while driving might seem harmless, but they require you to take at least one hand off the wheel, and spills can cause sudden distractions. Trying to grab a dropped item, wipe a stain, or adjust a lid while driving can quickly lead to losing control of your car. If you need to eat, it is best to do so when you are stopped at a rest area or parking lot rather than while in motion.

Music, podcasts, and audiobooks are common ways to pass the time while driving, but they should never be *so loud that you cannot hear what is happening around you*. Emergency sirens, car horns, and even unusual noises from your own vehicle are important cues that something is happening. Keeping the volume at a reasonable level and selecting playlists or stations before you start driving can help prevent unnecessary distractions.

Missouri's unpredictable weather can also add an element of distraction. Heavy rain, fog, or even bright sunlight can make it difficult to see, forcing you to adjust your focus constantly. Keeping sunglasses in your car for sunny days and making sure your windshield wipers are in good condition for rainy conditions can help reduce the need for sudden adjustments while driving.

Multitasking behind the wheel is a dangerous habit. Many drivers convince themselves that they can *text, eat, adjust settings, or even groom themselves* while driving without any issues, but the reality is that the human brain is not designed to focus on multiple tasks at once when operating a vehicle. Driving requires constant awareness of what is happening around you. A single second of inattention can mean the difference between safely arriving at your destination and being involved in an accident.

Staying fully engaged with the road means making a conscious effort to *minimize distractions and prioritize safety*. Before you start driving, putting your phone on *silent mode* or activating a *Do Not Disturb* feature can prevent unnecessary interruptions. Adjusting your seat, mirrors, climate controls, and navigation system before putting the car in motion can eliminate the need to make adjustments while driving. If something demands your attention—whether it is a ringing phone, a spilled drink, or a noisy passenger—the best solution is to pull over and handle it when you are stopped.

Fatigue and distractions are two of the biggest dangers on Missouri's roads, and both can be avoided by making smart choices. If you feel tired, you should not convince yourself that you can push through. Taking breaks, getting proper rest, and knowing your limits can keep you from becoming a hazard to yourself and others. If something distracts you, recognizing the risk and removing the distraction can prevent a moment of inattention from turning into a life-altering mistake. Safe driving is not just about following traffic laws—it is about being fully present and making responsible decisions every time you get behind the wheel.

4.5 HANDLING EMERGENCIES AND BREAKDOWNS

No matter how carefully you drive, emergencies can happen when you least expect them. A *blown tire, sudden engine failure, brake issues, or even an* accident can leave you in a stressful and potentially dangerous situation. Knowing exactly how to handle different types of roadside emergencies can make the difference between staying safe and putting yourself or others at risk. Missouri's highways, rural backroads, and busy city streets each present unique challenges when something goes wrong, and understanding how to respond properly is a crucial part of becoming a responsible driver.

If your car suddenly *breaks down* while you are driving, your first priority should be to get it off the road as safely as possible. If the engine is still running, gradually slow down and steer your vehicle toward the *right shoulder* or as far away from moving traffic as possible. Missouri law requires you to *use your hazard lights* immediately to alert other drivers that something is wrong. If your car is completely disabled and cannot be moved, remaining inside with your seatbelt on is often the safest option, especially on highways where traffic is moving at high speeds. Exiting your car in the middle of a busy road is extremely dangerous, so unless you are in immediate danger, it is best to wait for assistance inside your vehicle.

Carrying an *emergency kit* in your vehicle can make a significant difference in handling breakdowns. Items such as *reflective triangles, a flashlight, a spare tire, jumper cables, and a basic toolkit* can help you manage minor issues while waiting for help. If your car is stranded at night, placing reflective warning devices behind your vehicle can increase visibility and reduce the risk of another driver crashing into your stopped car. Road flares can also be useful in areas where lighting is poor, such as rural roads or highways without streetlights.

A *flat tire* is one of the most common roadside emergencies, and knowing how to change a tire can prevent long delays and costly towing fees. If you get a flat, steer your car to a safe location away from traffic and turn on your hazard lights. Make sure you are parked on level ground before attempting to change the tire. You should always use your parking brake to prevent your car from rolling. If you have a *spare tire, a jack, and a lug wrench*, you can replace the damaged tire by loosening the lug nuts, lifting the car with the jack, swapping the tire, and tightening the lug nuts securely. If you are unable to change the tire yourself, calling for roadside assistance is the safest option.

Brake failure is another dangerous situation that requires immediate action. If you press the brake pedal and *nothing happens*, remain calm and *do not panic*. The first thing you should try is *pumping the brake pedal rapidly* to build up any remaining brake pressure. If that does not work, you should slowly apply the *emergency brake (parking brake)* while keeping both hands firmly on the steering wheel. Shifting the car into a *lower gear* can also help slow you down, especially if you are driving an automatic vehicle with manual shifting options. If you are on a highway or a busy road, turning on your hazard lights and honking your horn can alert other drivers that your car is in distress. Your goal is to safely maneuver your car off the road and bring it to a stop without causing an accident.

Engine failure can occur for many reasons, but if your car *suddenly loses power* while driving, your first instinct may be to panic. Instead, you should *immediately take your foot off the accelerator* and begin steering toward a safe location. If your power steering goes out, turning the wheel may feel much harder, but you should still be able to control the car with extra effort. Once you have safely stopped, turning on your hazard lights will warn other drivers to slow down and give you space. If your car refuses to restart, calling for roadside assistance or a tow truck is usually your best option.

If your car's *engine overheats*, you may notice steam rising from the hood, a warning light on your dashboard, or an unusual burning smell. Overheating can happen on hot summer days in Missouri, especially if you are driving in stop-and-go traffic or climbing steep hills. If you notice signs of overheating, *pull over immediately* and turn off the engine. Opening the hood right away can be dangerous, as built-up pressure could cause hot coolant to spray out. Instead, you should wait at least *30 minutes* for the engine to cool down before checking fluid levels. If you have coolant in your car, carefully adding more may temporarily resolve the problem, but a mechanic should inspect the issue as soon as possible. Continuing to drive with an overheating engine can cause serious and expensive damage.

A *blown tire* is different from a normal flat tire and can be much more dangerous, especially at high speeds. If you hear a loud *bang* or feel the car *jerk suddenly*, your tire may have exploded. The worst thing you can do in this situation is slam on the brakes, as this can cause the car to lose control. Instead, *grip the steering wheel firmly* and allow the car to slow down gradually while steering toward the shoulder. Once your speed drops to a safe level, you can carefully brake and bring the vehicle to a complete stop.

If you ever find yourself involved in a *minor accident*, Missouri law requires you to *stop immediately*, even if the damage seems minimal. Leaving the scene of an accident can result in serious legal consequences. If possible, move your car out of the flow of traffic and turn on your hazard lights. You should check to see if anyone is injured and call emergency services if medical help is needed. Exchanging information with the other driver, including names, phone numbers, insurance details, and vehicle information, is essential. Taking *photos of the accident scene* can help with insurance claims and provide evidence if there are any disputes.

For *major accidents* where injuries are involved or vehicles are severely damaged, you should call *911* right away and remain at the scene until law enforcement arrives. You should never admit fault at the scene of an accident, as determining responsibility is the job of insurance companies and law enforcement officials. If possible, staying in your car with your seatbelt on until help arrives is often the safest option, especially if you are on a busy highway or in dangerous conditions.

Wildlife-related crashes are a real danger in Missouri, particularly in rural areas where deer crossings are common. If a deer suddenly appears in front of your vehicle, your natural instinct may be to *swerve*, but this can be more dangerous than hitting the animal. Swerving can lead to losing control of your car and crashing into trees, guardrails, or other vehicles. Instead, if a collision is unavoidable, it is safer to *brake firmly and stay in your lane*. If you do hit an animal, pulling over and checking for damage is important, but you should never attempt to move a large injured animal yourself, as it could be dangerous.

During winter months, Missouri roads can become slick with *snow and ice*, increasing the chances of skidding or losing control. If your car begins to skid, your instinct might be to slam on the brakes, but this can make the situation worse. Instead, *take your foot off the accelerator and steer in the direction you want to go*. If you are driving a vehicle with *anti-lock brakes (ABS)*, you should apply steady pressure to the brake pedal. If you do not have ABS, *pumping the brakes gently* can help prevent the wheels from locking up.

Being prepared for emergencies means knowing how to respond calmly and safely. Keeping your car well-maintained, checking fluid levels, tire pressure, and brakes regularly, and always carrying an emergency kit can reduce the chances of experiencing a breakdown. If something does go wrong, staying aware of your surroundings, using your hazard lights, and making smart decisions about when and where to stop can keep you safe. Roadside emergencies are unpredictable, but having the right knowledge and preparation will help you handle them with confidence and caution.

CHAPTER 5
VEHICLE CONTROL AND OPERATION

5.1 BASIC VEHICLE CONTROLS AND INSTRUMENTATION

Before you can safely drive on Missouri roads, you must become familiar with the *basic vehicle controls and instrumentation* that allow you to operate a car effectively. Whether you are navigating through city traffic, merging onto a highway, or making a routine stop at a traffic light, understanding how your vehicle functions is essential for making split-second decisions and responding to different driving situations. Every car may have slight variations in design and layout, but the fundamental controls remain the same. By knowing exactly where each control is located and how it works, you will be able to drive with confidence and avoid unnecessary distractions.

When you first sit in the driver's seat, the most important thing you should do is *adjust your seat, mirrors, and steering wheel* to ensure maximum comfort and visibility. Your seat should be positioned so that you can *easily reach the pedals* without stretching and maintain a clear view of the road. The rearview and side mirrors should be set to *eliminate as many blind spots as possible* and provide a full picture of the surrounding traffic. A properly adjusted steering wheel should allow you to steer without strain while keeping both hands in a comfortable position.

The *steering wheel* is your primary tool for controlling the direction of the car. Modern vehicles are equipped with *power steering*, which makes turning the wheel much easier than in older cars. When making small adjustments to stay in your lane or navigate a turn, you should always keep *both hands on the wheel* in a position that allows for quick and precise movements. The traditional hand placement of *10 and 2 o'clock* has shifted to *9 and 3 o'clock* in many driving guidelines to reduce injury risk if an airbag deploys. When turning, using a *hand-over-hand technique* allows for better control, while allowing the wheel to slide back through your hands smoothly after completing the turn ensures stability.

Your *accelerator (gas pedal) and brake pedal* are the most frequently used controls while driving. The accelerator is responsible for increasing speed, while the brake pedal allows you to slow down or stop. You should always *use your right foot* for both pedals to avoid confusion or accidental pressing of both at the same time. When pressing the accelerator, applying gentle and steady pressure allows for smoother acceleration, which is particularly important in heavy traffic or on slippery roads. The brake pedal should be pressed gradually, as *sudden or harsh braking* can cause the vehicle to skid or cause discomfort for passengers. Some vehicles are equipped with *anti-lock braking systems (ABS)*, which prevent the wheels from locking up during sudden stops. If your car has ABS, pressing the brake firmly and maintaining pressure will allow the system to work effectively.

The *gear shift* is another crucial component of vehicle control. Most cars in Missouri today are *automatic*, meaning the car selects the appropriate gear for driving. However, you still need to be familiar with the different settings, which typically include *Park (P), Reverse (R), Neutral (N), and Drive (D)*. Some automatic vehicles also have *low gear settings (L1, L2)* for better control when driving on steep inclines or slippery conditions. In contrast, if you are driving a *manual transmission* vehicle, you will need to learn how to use a *clutch pedal* in combination with the gear shift to manually change gears. Manual cars require more skill and practice, as improper shifting can cause the engine to stall.

Your *dashboard instrumentation* provides critical information about your vehicle's performance and potential problems. The most important gauge is the *speedometer*, which shows how fast you are traveling. In Missouri, different roads have specific *speed limits*, and exceeding them can result in traffic violations or accidents. Next to the speedometer, you will often find the *odometer*, which tracks the total distance your vehicle has traveled. This is useful for maintenance schedules, as certain services, like oil changes and tire rotations, are recommended after a specific number of miles.

The *fuel gauge* is another important indicator, showing how much gas is left in the tank. Running out of fuel on the road can be dangerous, especially in rural areas where gas stations may be far apart. Many newer vehicles have *low fuel warning lights* that activate when the gas level reaches a critical point. If this light turns on, you should plan to refuel as soon as possible. The *temperature gauge* monitors your engine's heat levels, and if it moves into the red zone, it means the engine is overheating. Driving with an overheated engine can cause serious damage, so you should pull over immediately and let the car cool down before checking coolant levels.

The *check engine light* is one of the most commonly misunderstood warning indicators. While it does not always signal an emergency, ignoring it can lead to costly repairs. If the light comes on and stays solid, it typically indicates a minor issue, such as a loose gas cap or a sensor problem. However, if it starts *flashing*, this could mean a more serious malfunction that requires immediate attention. Other important dashboard indicators include the *battery light*, which warns of electrical problems, and the *oil pressure light*, which signals issues with engine lubrication.

Understanding your *turn signals, headlights, and windshield wipers* is also essential for safe driving. The *turn signal lever* is usually located on the left side of the steering column. Pushing it up signals a *right turn*, while pushing it down signals a *left turn*. Missouri law requires drivers to *use turn signals at least 100 feet* before making a turn or changing lanes. Failing to do so can result in a traffic violation and increase the risk of an accident.

Your *headlights* not only help you see in low-visibility conditions but also make your car visible to other drivers. In Missouri, you must use your headlights *from 30 minutes after sunset until 30 minutes before sunrise*, as well as during fog, heavy rain, or any time visibility is reduced to less than 500 feet. Most vehicles have different headlight settings, including *low beams and high beams*. High beams should only be used in areas with no oncoming traffic, as they can blind other drivers. If another car's high beams are shining directly at you, looking slightly to the right of the road can reduce glare and help you maintain focus.

Your *windshield wipers* are controlled by a lever that typically has multiple speed settings. Rain and snow can significantly reduce visibility, making properly functioning wipers essential. Missouri law requires you to use your headlights whenever your windshield wipers are in use due to rain or snow. Keeping an adequate supply of *windshield washer fluid* is also important, as dirt and debris can quickly accumulate on the windshield, obstructing your view.

Your *emergency brake (parking brake)* provides extra security when parking on hills or steep surfaces. In automatic cars, shifting into *Park (P)* alone may not be enough to keep the vehicle from rolling, so engaging the emergency brake adds an extra layer of stability. In manual transmission vehicles, the emergency brake is essential for preventing rollback when starting from a stop on an incline.

In addition to the main controls, modern cars are equipped with *advanced driver-assistance systems (ADAS)* designed to enhance safety. Features such as *lane departure warnings, adaptive cruise control, blind-spot monitoring, and automatic emergency braking* help prevent accidents by providing alerts or taking corrective actions. While these technologies are helpful, they should never replace your attention and responsibility as a driver. You must always remain fully engaged and aware of your surroundings, regardless of how many automated features your car has.

Being familiar with your vehicle's controls and instrumentation will not only help you pass your Missouri permit test but will also make you a safer, more confident driver. Before taking your car on the road, spending time getting comfortable with each control, practicing smooth braking and acceleration, and regularly checking your dashboard indicators will ensure that you are prepared for any driving situation. Developing good habits early on will make operating your vehicle feel natural, allowing you to focus on the road ahead with full control and awareness.

5.2 STEERING TECHNIQUES AND HAND POSITIONS

Steering is the foundation of vehicle control, and mastering the correct *steering techniques and hand positions* is essential for safe driving. Your ability to steer effectively will determine how well you navigate turns, maintain lane position, and respond to unexpected situations. Every movement of the steering wheel should be smooth, deliberate, and controlled, as sudden jerks or overcorrections can cause the vehicle to veer off course or lose traction, especially on wet or icy roads. Whether you are making a slight lane adjustment on the highway, executing a tight turn on a city street, or maneuvering through a parking lot, knowing exactly how to position your hands and how to move the wheel will make you a more confident and precise driver.

Your *hand placement on the steering wheel* directly affects how much control you have over the vehicle. Traditionally, many drivers were taught to keep their hands at the *10 and 2 o'clock* positions, mimicking the hands of a clock. However, safety experts, including the Missouri Department of Revenue and national traffic safety organizations, now recommend positioning your hands at *9 and 3 o'clock* instead. This lower hand placement gives you better steering control and reduces the risk of serious injury if the airbag deploys. Airbags inflate with extreme force in a crash, and if your hands are too high, they can be pushed back into your face upon impact. The *9 and 3 o'clock* position also allows for a more natural arm posture, reducing fatigue during long drives and providing better leverage when making turns.

When *turning the steering wheel*, there are different techniques you can use depending on the type of turn and how much precision is needed. One of the most effective methods for general driving is the *push-pull technique*, sometimes referred to as *hand-to-hand steering*. In this technique, one hand pushes the wheel up while the other hand pulls it down in a coordinated motion, allowing for smooth and controlled steering without crossing your arms. This method is particularly useful for gradual turns, lane changes, and minor adjustments, as it keeps both hands in contact with the wheel at all times, providing maximum control.

For sharper turns, such as making a right or left turn at an intersection, the *hand-over-hand technique* can be more effective. This method involves one hand crossing over the other as you pull the wheel in the desired direction. While this allows for quicker and more extreme steering inputs, it requires careful coordination to prevent oversteering. If you use this technique, you should allow the wheel to smoothly return to the center position after the turn, rather than letting it snap back on its own. Maintaining steady control ensures that you don't lose balance in the steering, which is especially important when driving on curvy roads or dealing with sudden changes in traffic.

One-handed steering should generally be avoided unless necessary. There may be moments when you need to briefly remove a hand to operate another vehicle function, such as adjusting windshield wipers or shifting gears in a manual transmission, but you should always return both hands to the wheel as soon as possible. Driving with one hand, especially with a relaxed grip at the bottom of the wheel, reduces your ability to react quickly in an emergency and increases the likelihood of losing control. Some drivers develop a habit of steering with only a few fingers or resting a hand on the top of the wheel, but these positions offer little stability and make it difficult to respond to sudden movements or road hazards.

Your grip on the steering wheel should be *firm but not too tight*. A relaxed grip allows you to make smooth adjustments without unnecessary tension in your hands and arms. Gripping the wheel too tightly can cause fatigue and make steering movements less fluid, which is particularly noticeable on long drives or in stop-and-go traffic. If your hands feel strained after driving for a while, it may be a sign that you are gripping the wheel too hard. Keeping your wrists flexible and making small, gentle movements will give you better control over the vehicle without excessive effort.

Steering sensitivity varies from one vehicle to another. Some cars have a very responsive steering system that requires only slight movements to change direction, while others may require more effort to turn. It's important to familiarize yourself with how your specific vehicle responds to steering input. If you are driving a new or unfamiliar car, testing the wheel's responsiveness in a safe, open area before entering traffic will help you get a feel for its handling.

When driving at higher speeds, such as on highways or interstates, steering should be *light and precise*. Making sudden or exaggerated movements at high speeds can cause the car to become unstable, especially in strong crosswinds or when passing large vehicles like trucks and buses. Keeping both hands firmly in place and making small, controlled adjustments will help maintain a straight path without unnecessary swerving.

When driving at lower speeds, such as in parking lots or residential areas, you may need to make more exaggerated turns. Parking maneuvers, U-turns, and sharp corners require you to turn the wheel more, and this is where the *hand-over-hand technique* can be useful. However, when making very slow maneuvers, such as backing into a parking space, you may need to briefly use *one-handed steering* to look over your shoulder while reversing. Even in these situations, you should keep at least one hand in a stable position on the wheel and be prepared to return both hands to *9 and 3 o'clock* once the maneuver is complete.

In Missouri, you are required to *signal at least 100 feet* before making a turn or lane change, and steering plays a critical role in executing these movements safely. When merging into another lane, you should make a *gradual, smooth steering movement* rather than a sharp or sudden motion. A slow, steady adjustment allows other drivers to anticipate your movement and react accordingly. Quick, jerky lane changes can startle other drivers and increase the risk of an accident, especially on multi-lane roads with heavy traffic.

When making left or right turns at intersections, you should steer in a controlled motion that keeps your vehicle in the correct lane throughout the turn. Turning too early or too sharply can cause you to drift into another lane or hit the curb, while turning too late can cause you to swing too wide and enter oncoming traffic. Practicing turns at different speeds and angles will help you develop a sense of how much steering input is needed for each type of turn.

Driving in Missouri also means encountering different road conditions, from winding rural highways to busy city streets. On narrow roads, especially those with little or no shoulder space, you should *steer carefully to maintain lane position* while avoiding hazards like potholes or debris. On wet or icy roads, steering must be even more controlled, as sudden movements can cause the tires to lose traction. If your car starts to skid, you should *steer gently in the direction you want to go* rather than overcorrecting, which can make the skid worse.

If you ever need to make an *emergency maneuver*, such as swerving to avoid an obstacle, your steering technique is crucial. Overreacting with sudden, forceful steering can cause the vehicle to fishtail or roll over, especially in vehicles with a high center of gravity. The best way to handle an emergency is to *look where you want to go, keep both hands on the wheel, and steer in a controlled manner* to avoid losing balance.

Mastering *steering techniques and hand positions* is one of the most important aspects of becoming a safe and skilled driver. The way you steer affects every part of your driving experience, from making routine turns to handling unexpected hazards. By practicing smooth, controlled movements and keeping both hands in the correct position, you will build confidence and precision on the road. Developing good steering habits early on will make driving feel more natural and allow you to respond calmly and effectively in any situation.

5.3 ACCELERATION, BRAKING, AND STOPPING DISTANCES

Controlling the speed of your vehicle is one of the most fundamental skills you will develop as a driver. Every time you press the accelerator or brake pedal, you are making a decision that affects not only your own movement but also the movement of everyone around you. *Acceleration, braking, and stopping distances* determine how smoothly you drive, how safely you interact with other vehicles, and how effectively you can respond to sudden changes in road conditions. These actions may seem simple at first—pressing one pedal to go faster and another to slow down—but each movement requires careful judgment, an understanding of how your car responds, and an awareness of the environment around you.

When you press the *accelerator pedal*, your car's engine increases its power output, allowing the vehicle to move forward or gain speed. Acceleration should always be *smooth and controlled*, not sudden or jerky. A common mistake new drivers make is pressing too hard on the accelerator, causing the car to lurch forward. This can be dangerous in traffic, as it makes it harder to maintain a safe following distance and can lead to loss of control, especially on slippery roads. Light, gradual pressure is always the safest way to accelerate.

The amount of acceleration you need depends on several factors, including road conditions, traffic flow, and the power of your vehicle's engine. If you are driving on a flat road with no traffic, gentle acceleration is usually enough to reach your desired speed. However, if you are merging onto a highway, you will need to accelerate more quickly to match the speed of moving traffic. Missouri highways, like I-70 and I-44, have on-ramps designed to give you enough space to accelerate before merging, but you must judge the speed of vehicles in the right lane and adjust accordingly.

When driving uphill, your car will naturally slow down due to gravity, so you may need to apply more acceleration to maintain speed. Conversely, when going downhill, gravity will make your car gain speed even without pressing the accelerator. In these situations, you should ease off the pedal and be ready to *apply the brakes gently* if necessary to keep your speed under control. Speed limit signs on steep downhill roads, such as those found in the Ozark Mountains or near the Missouri River bluffs, often remind drivers to reduce speed for safety.

Braking is just as important as accelerating, if not more so. Pressing the *brake pedal* slows your vehicle by reducing wheel rotation and creating friction between the brake pads and rotors. Like acceleration, braking should always be done in a *smooth, controlled manner.* Slamming on the brakes suddenly can cause your car to skid, especially on wet or icy roads. It also increases the risk of a rear-end collision, as drivers behind you may not have enough time to react. The best way to brake safely is to *apply steady, even pressure* on the pedal, gradually reducing your speed instead of stopping abruptly.

Most modern vehicles in Missouri are equipped with *antilock braking systems (ABS)*, which prevent the wheels from locking up during hard braking. If you need to stop suddenly, ABS allows you to press the brake pedal firmly while still maintaining steering control. Without ABS, hard braking can cause the wheels to lock up, making it difficult to steer and increasing the risk of skidding. If your car does not have ABS, you should use a technique called *threshold braking*, which involves pressing the brake pedal firmly but not so hard that the wheels lock up. If you feel them start to skid, ease off the brake slightly to regain control.

The *stopping distance* of your vehicle is the total distance it takes to come to a complete stop after recognizing a need to slow down. Stopping distance is affected by three main factors: *perception distance, reaction distance, and braking distance. Perception distance* is the distance your car travels while you recognize the need to stop. *Reaction distance* is the distance your car moves while you physically react by moving your foot from the accelerator to the brake. *Braking distance* is the actual distance required to bring the vehicle to a full stop after pressing the brake pedal. Together, these three factors determine how much space you need to stop safely.

At 55 mph, the average stopping distance on dry pavement is about *265 feet*, or nearly the length of a football field. This means if you are following another vehicle too closely, you may not have enough room to stop in time if they suddenly hit the brakes. Following too closely, also known as *tailgating*, is one of the most common causes of rear-end collisions. To maintain a safe following distance, you should use the *three-second rule*, which means staying at least three seconds behind the vehicle in front of you. On wet or icy roads, you should increase this to at least five seconds, as reduced traction increases your stopping distance.

Different road conditions can significantly affect how your vehicle accelerates and stops. On dry pavement, your tires have the most grip, allowing for normal acceleration and braking. However, on *wet roads*, water reduces tire traction, increasing the risk of hydroplaning. If you accelerate too quickly on wet pavement, your tires may spin, and if you brake too hard, your car may skid. To avoid hydroplaning, drive at a steady speed and avoid sudden movements. On *snow or ice*, stopping distances can be up to ten times longer than on dry roads. You should *accelerate and brake gently* to prevent skidding, and if your car starts to slide, steer in the direction you want to go while easing off the brake.

Another factor that affects stopping distance is *vehicle weight.* Heavier vehicles require more time to slow down because of their momentum. A small car will generally stop more quickly than a large SUV or truck. If you are driving a fully loaded vehicle or pulling a trailer, you should allow extra time to brake, as the added weight increases the strain on your braking system. Missouri's roads include many areas with steep inclines, particularly in rural regions, so drivers pulling heavy loads must be especially cautious when braking downhill to avoid overheating the brakes.

Proper vehicle maintenance also plays a crucial role in acceleration and braking performance. Worn-out brake pads, low tire tread, or underinflated tires can increase stopping distance and make it harder to control your vehicle. Checking your brakes and tires regularly ensures that they are in good condition and function properly when needed. In Missouri, vehicle safety inspections include checking the brake system to ensure it meets state requirements. If your brakes make a squeaking or grinding noise, it may be a sign that the brake pads need replacing.

Night driving and poor visibility conditions also impact how you accelerate and brake. At night, your ability to judge speed and distance is reduced, making it even more important to leave extra space between you and the car ahead. Fog, rain, and snow further limit visibility, which means you may not see a hazard in time to stop safely. Slowing down, increasing following distance, and using low-beam headlights in foggy conditions can help you stay in control.

Emergency braking situations require quick thinking and controlled movements. If you encounter a sudden obstacle, such as a deer crossing the road—a common occurrence in Missouri, particularly in wooded areas—you must decide whether to brake hard, steer around it, or both. Swerving suddenly at high speeds can be just as dangerous as braking too hard, so you must judge the safest course of action based on your surroundings.

Mastering *acceleration, braking, and stopping distances* is essential for safe driving. Smooth and controlled speed adjustments make the driving experience more comfortable, prevent unnecessary wear on your vehicle, and reduce the risk of accidents. Understanding how different road conditions affect stopping distance allows you to anticipate hazards and adjust accordingly. With practice, you will develop the ability to make split-second decisions that keep you and others safe on the road.

5.4 PARKING METHODS: PARALLEL, PERPENDICULAR, AND ANGLE

Parking is a skill that requires precision, patience, and a clear understanding of how your vehicle moves. Whether you are pulling into a spot at a shopping centre, parallel parking on a busy street in Kansas City, or navigating angled spaces in a public lot, knowing how to position your car correctly is essential. Each parking method—*parallel, perpendicular, and angle parking*—has its own technique, challenges, and rules. Mastering these techniques will not only make parking easier but also help you avoid accidents, fines, and unnecessary stress when driving in Missouri.

Parallel parking is often seen as the most difficult of the three because it requires precise control over steering, braking, and acceleration while maneuvering your car into a tight space between two parked vehicles. In Missouri, this skill is especially important because it is a requirement for the driving test. When parallel parking, the first step is to find a space that is at least one and a half times the length of your vehicle. This gives you enough room to maneuver safely without scraping the curb or hitting the car in front or behind you.

Once you have found a suitable space, you should pull up beside the car in front of the spot, aligning your rear bumper with its rear bumper. This positioning is crucial because it sets you up for a smooth entry into the space. Next, you should shift into reverse and begin turning your steering wheel sharply toward the curb while slowly backing up. As your car starts to move into the space, you need to carefully adjust your steering to straighten out. The key is to keep your movements slow and controlled. If your front end is too far out into the road, you can pull forward slightly to correct your position.

Missouri law requires that when you are parallel parked, your car should be no more than 18 inches from the curb. If your tires are too far from the curb, you may need to reposition by pulling forward and reversing again. It is also important to check your mirrors and blind spots before opening your door to exit the vehicle, especially in high-traffic areas. Cities like St. Louis and Springfield have many narrow streets where parallel parking is common, so practicing in a low-traffic area before attempting it in a busy location can help build confidence.

Perpendicular parking is one of the most common parking methods, used in most parking lots at grocery stores, schools, and office buildings. The goal is to position your car neatly between two lines that mark the space. This type of parking can be done by either pulling forward into a spot or reversing into it, with each method having its advantages. Pulling forward into a space is easier for new drivers because it requires less steering control, but it can make it harder to see approaching traffic when backing out. Reversing into a space takes a bit more practice, but it allows for an easier and safer exit when leaving.

When pulling into a perpendicular spot, you should approach slowly and start turning your steering wheel when your front bumper aligns with the edge of the space. Turning too early can cause you to cross over into the next parking space, while turning too late might not give you enough room to straighten out. Your goal is to enter the space smoothly, with your car centered between the two lines. If you find that one side of your car is too close to another vehicle, you may need to back out slightly and readjust.

Backing into a perpendicular space follows a similar process but in reverse. You should position your car so that its rear bumper is slightly past the space before beginning to turn. Looking over your shoulder and checking your mirrors frequently is important to ensure you do not hit anything. Many parking lots in Missouri have designated "reverse parking only" sections, as this method is considered safer when exiting.

Angle parking is often used in smaller parking lots, public parks, and along some streets in smaller towns throughout Missouri. The spaces are designed at an angle, usually 30 to 60 degrees, making it easier to pull in and out without needing to turn sharply. This type of parking is simpler than perpendicular parking because it requires less maneuvering, but it still requires careful attention to positioning.

When approaching an angled parking space, you should slow down and begin turning when your front bumper reaches the midpoint of the space. This ensures that your vehicle enters smoothly without cutting into the next spot. Because the spaces are designed at an angle, reversing out can be more challenging than reversing from a perpendicular space. You need to check your surroundings carefully before backing up to avoid hitting pedestrians or oncoming vehicles. Some Missouri towns have angle parking on main roads, which means that when backing out, you are reversing directly into traffic. In these situations, it is essential to back out slowly while checking both directions for approaching cars.

No matter which parking method you use, Missouri law has several important parking regulations that you must follow. It is illegal to park in front of driveways, within intersections, or too close to fire hydrants. If you are parking on a hill, you should turn your wheels toward the curb when parking downhill and away from the curb when parking uphill. This prevents your car from rolling into traffic if your brakes fail. Using your parking brake in these situations adds an extra layer of safety.

Missouri also has specific rules about disabled parking spaces. These spaces are reserved for individuals with disabilities and require a valid disabled parking placard or license plate. Parking in one of these spaces without proper authorization can result in fines and penalties.

Parking in busy areas, such as near stadiums during a Kansas City Chiefs or St. Louis Cardinals game, requires extra patience. In these crowded environments, finding a space can be difficult, and navigating through pedestrians and other vehicles demands full attention. Practicing different parking methods in a quiet lot before driving in high-traffic areas can help you build the skills needed to park confidently.

In some situations, parking can be restricted based on the time of day. Certain streets in urban areas have metered parking, where you must pay a fee to park for a limited period. These meters are often monitored closely, and failing to pay or exceeding the time limit can result in a parking ticket. Reading parking signs carefully is important to avoid fines and ensure you are legally parked.

Understanding the different parking methods and how to apply them in real-world situations makes you a more capable and responsible driver. By practicing parallel parking for urban environments, perfecting perpendicular parking for everyday lots, and mastering angle parking for smaller spaces, you will be prepared for any parking challenge Missouri roads present. Confidently maneuvering your vehicle into a space is not just about skill—it is about safety, awareness, and following the rules of the road.

CHAPTER 6
MISSOURI'S ROADWAY ENVIRONMENTS

6.1 URBAN DRIVING: NAVIGATING CITY STREETS

Driving through a city like St. Louis or Kansas City requires a completely different set of skills than driving on a quiet country road. The streets are often crowded, lanes are tightly packed, and there is always something demanding your attention—whether it's a traffic light changing ahead, a pedestrian stepping onto a crosswalk, or a vehicle suddenly pulling out from a parallel parking spot. Navigating through Missouri's urban areas successfully means knowing how to handle these challenges with confidence while keeping yourself, your passengers, and those around you safe.

Traffic signals are one of the most important aspects of urban driving, and understanding how to respond to them quickly is crucial. In Missouri, you will encounter standard red, yellow, and green lights, but city intersections often include additional signals such as protected left-turn arrows, flashing yellow arrows, and pedestrian crossing signals. Knowing when you can safely turn at a red light is just as important as recognizing when a yellow light means you should slow down instead of trying to rush through before it turns red. At intersections with multiple lanes, there may be lane-specific signals that indicate whether you can continue straight, turn left, or turn right. Many city intersections also have cameras that monitor for red-light violations, and running a red light in Missouri can result in a fine or even points on your driving record.

Pedestrians and cyclists are much more common in urban areas, and Missouri law prioritizes their safety in traffic situations. At crosswalks, pedestrians always have the right of way, meaning you must stop and allow them to cross before proceeding. This is especially important in busy downtown areas where people are walking between office buildings, restaurants, and shops. Some intersections have *pedestrian scramble signals*, which stop all traffic in all directions and allow pedestrians to cross however they need to, including diagonally. Cyclists are also a frequent presence in Missouri's cities, and you need to be aware of bike lanes, which are often marked with painted symbols or green pavement. If you are turning right across a bike lane, you must yield to any cyclists traveling in the same direction. When passing a cyclist on a city street, Missouri law requires that you leave at least three feet of space between your vehicle and the cyclist.

Lane management in urban settings can be complex, especially during rush hour. Many city streets have *dedicated lanes* for buses, bicycles, or turning vehicles, and failing to stay in the correct lane can lead to confusion or even a traffic violation. Some lanes operate differently at different times of the day, meaning that a lane used for parking in the morning might be an active driving lane during the afternoon rush. Overhead lane-use signs or digital signals are common on larger roads and highways in cities, and you must pay attention to them to ensure you are in the correct lane for your destination.

Merging and lane changes require extra caution in heavy traffic, where drivers may not always be willing to make space for you. When merging into a busy street from a parking lot or side road, you should always look for a safe gap in traffic rather than forcing your way in. If you need to change lanes, use your turn signal well in advance so that other drivers can anticipate your movement. Checking your mirrors is important, but you should also glance over your shoulder to check your *blind spots*, as vehicles in the adjacent lane might not always be visible in your mirrors.

Speed limits in Missouri's urban areas are often lower than on highways or rural roads. In most city settings, the speed limit is 25 to 35 mph unless otherwise posted, but certain areas, such as school zones, require even lower speeds. Flashing yellow school zone signs indicate when reduced speed limits are in effect, and driving too fast in these areas can result in higher fines and penalties. Construction zones also require lower speeds, even if workers are not currently present, and Missouri law doubles fines for speeding in work zones.

Traffic congestion is a daily reality in Missouri's cities, especially during morning and evening rush hours. Gridlock can be frustrating, but aggressive driving or constantly switching lanes will not get you to your destination any faster. Keeping a safe following distance is critical, as stop-and-go traffic can result in sudden braking. Rear-end collisions are one of the most common types of accidents in urban driving, and Missouri law considers the driver in the rear to be at fault in most cases. To avoid being involved in one, you should follow the *three-second rule*, which means keeping at least three seconds of space between your vehicle and the car in front of you. This gives you enough time to react if the vehicle ahead suddenly stops.

Parking and stopping regulations are stricter in urban areas than in suburban or rural settings. Many streets have *metered parking*, requiring you to pay for a set amount of time, and exceeding your time limit can result in a fine. Some meters allow payment through mobile apps, while others require coins or credit cards. In some areas, parking is restricted during certain hours to allow for street cleaning or delivery trucks, and failing to follow posted regulations can lead to your car being towed. Double parking—stopping next to a parked car and blocking traffic—is illegal and can cause serious traffic disruptions. If you need to stop briefly to drop off a passenger, look for designated *loading zones* rather than blocking a traffic lane.

One-way streets are common in downtown areas, and it is important to recognize them to avoid driving in the wrong direction. Signs indicating one-way streets are usually posted at intersections, but you can also look at the direction that parked cars are facing to confirm the flow of traffic. Many one-way streets have multiple lanes, and you should always stay in the lane that aligns with your intended direction of travel. When making a turn onto a one-way street, be sure to turn into the correct lane rather than cutting across multiple lanes.

Emergency vehicles are a frequent presence in urban settings, and knowing how to respond to them correctly is essential. If you hear a siren or see flashing lights approaching from behind, you must pull over to the right and stop if possible. If you are in heavy traffic and pulling over is not an option, remain where you are but avoid blocking intersections so that emergency vehicles can pass through. Fire stations, hospitals, and police stations are common in city areas, meaning you may encounter emergency vehicles more frequently than in rural settings.

Public transportation adds another layer of complexity to urban driving. In Missouri's major cities, buses often stop in traffic lanes to pick up and drop off passengers, and you must be prepared to stop or change lanes safely when encountering one. Some intersections have *bus-only signals*, allowing buses to proceed before general traffic, and you must follow these signals even if the main traffic light is green. In areas where streetcars or light rail systems operate, you should always yield to them, as they cannot swerve or stop quickly to avoid a collision.

Weather conditions can make urban driving even more challenging, especially during Missouri's unpredictable winters. Snow and ice can create slippery road conditions, making it harder to stop at intersections or navigate turns. Bridges and overpasses freeze first, and black ice can be nearly invisible. Rain can reduce visibility and increase braking distances, especially on roads with worn pavement. Adjusting your speed, increasing your following distance, and using your headlights in low-visibility conditions will help you stay safe when driving in the city during bad weather.

Adapting to the fast-paced environment of city driving takes practice, but by developing strong observation skills, staying patient in heavy traffic, and being prepared for unexpected situations, you will be able to navigate Missouri's urban streets with confidence. Every intersection, lane change, and parking decision requires awareness and quick thinking, and by applying these skills, you will become a safer and more efficient driver in any city setting.

6.2 RURAL DRIVING: CHALLENGES OF COUNTRY ROADS

Driving on Missouri's rural roads presents an entirely different set of challenges compared to navigating the busy streets of its cities. While the absence of heavy traffic might make country roads seem peaceful and uncomplicated, the reality is that these roads require just as much—if not more—focus and skill than urban driving. The conditions can be unpredictable, the terrain varies widely, and the lack of clear markings or lighting can make even familiar routes dangerous if you are not careful.

Narrow roads are one of the first things you will notice when driving in rural Missouri. Unlike multi-lane highways or city streets with clearly defined shoulders, many country roads are barely wide enough for two vehicles to pass each other comfortably. Some are paved but lack lane markings, while others may be gravel or even dirt, making traction more difficult, especially after rain or snow. When encountering another vehicle on a narrow road, slowing down and keeping as far to the right as possible is essential. If there isn't enough room for both vehicles to pass safely, one driver may need to pull off onto the shoulder or into a wider section of the road to allow the other to pass.

Blind curves and hills are common on Missouri's rural highways, especially in areas like the Ozarks, where the landscape is hilly and winding. These features reduce visibility, making it difficult to see oncoming traffic or obstacles in the road. If you are approaching a curve with no clear view ahead, reducing your speed is the safest option. In some cases, advisory speed limit signs will indicate how fast you should go around a curve, but even if no sign is present, slowing down gives you more time to react. On steep hills, your ability to see what's ahead may be blocked by the crest of the road. If you are driving uphill, always assume there may be a slow-moving vehicle or even an animal just beyond your line of sight. Staying to the right and maintaining a controlled speed will help prevent dangerous situations.

Unpaved and gravel roads make up a large portion of Missouri's rural transportation network. These roads can be tricky to navigate because they offer less traction than paved surfaces, increasing the risk of skidding or losing control, especially when braking or turning. Gravel roads also tend to develop *ruts* and *washboards*—uneven sections caused by repeated vehicle use—that can make steering more difficult. If you are driving on gravel, keeping a firm grip on the wheel and avoiding sudden movements is important. Slamming on the brakes or making sharp turns can cause your vehicle to slide, and if the road is wet, it may feel as slippery as ice.

Wildlife crossings are a major concern on rural roads, particularly at dawn and dusk when animals like deer are most active. Missouri is home to a large deer population, and collisions between vehicles and deer are not uncommon. In wooded areas or near open fields, it's best to remain extra vigilant, scanning the sides of the road for any movement. Deer often travel in groups, so if you see one, more may be nearby. If an animal suddenly appears in front of your vehicle, braking firmly is usually the best response—swerving can be dangerous because it may lead you into oncoming traffic or off the road entirely.

Farm equipment is another common sight on Missouri's country roads. Tractors, combines, and other large agricultural vehicles often move slowly and take up more than one lane, especially on roads without shoulders. Unlike city traffic, where slow-moving vehicles are rare, rural drivers must be prepared to adjust their speed when encountering farm machinery. Most farm vehicles will have bright orange *slow-moving vehicle* signs on the back, alerting you to their reduced speed. Passing a tractor or combine requires patience, as these vehicles may not be able to move out of your way immediately. Only pass when it is safe, and never assume the driver can see you approaching.

Railroad crossings without signals are common in Missouri's rural areas, where smaller roads intersect with train tracks. Unlike city crossings that have flashing lights and gates, many country crossings rely only on a stop sign or a crossbuck sign to warn drivers. This means you must take extra precautions before crossing. Slowing down, looking both ways, and listening for an approaching train are crucial steps. Because trains in rural areas often travel at high speeds, assuming the tracks are clear can be a deadly mistake. Some crossings also have multiple tracks, meaning that even if one train has passed, another could be coming from the opposite direction.

Lack of streetlights is another factor that makes rural driving more challenging, especially at night. Unlike cities, where bright lights illuminate intersections and roadways, country roads can be completely dark apart from your vehicle's headlights. This can make it harder to judge distances, spot obstacles, or see turns ahead. Using your high beams when there is no oncoming traffic will help you see farther down the road, but you should always dim them when approaching another vehicle to avoid blinding the driver.

Emergency response times in rural areas are often longer than in urban settings. If an accident or breakdown occurs, it may take emergency services more time to reach you, so being prepared is essential. Having a fully charged phone, a flashlight, and extra supplies like water, blankets, and a first-aid kit can make a big difference if you find yourself stranded. Additionally, some areas in Missouri have weak or no cell signal, which means you may not be able to call for help right away. Knowing your route in advance and telling someone your expected arrival time can provide an extra layer of safety.

Bridges and low-water crossings present another challenge unique to rural Missouri. Many backroads feature small, older bridges that may not have guardrails or clear weight limits posted. In areas prone to heavy rain, low-water crossings can become dangerous quickly. These are sections of the road where water flows over the pavement instead of under a bridge. While they may appear shallow, even a few inches of water can sweep a vehicle off the road. If you encounter a flooded crossing, never attempt to drive through it—turn around and find an alternate route.

Speed limits on rural roads in Missouri vary but are generally higher than in city environments. Many state highways in rural areas have speed limits of 55 mph, while smaller county roads may have lower limits posted. However, just because the speed limit is higher does not mean it is always safe to drive at that speed. Curves, loose gravel, and unexpected obstacles can make high speeds dangerous. Adjusting your speed based on road conditions is just as important as following posted limits.

Passing on rural roads requires extra caution due to limited visibility and the potential for oncoming traffic. Some two-lane highways have designated *passing zones*, marked by dashed yellow lines, indicating where it is safe to pass another vehicle. Solid yellow lines indicate *no-passing zones*, often because of hills, curves, or intersections ahead. Even when passing is legal, you must ensure you have enough space to safely complete the maneuver without cutting too close to the vehicle you are passing or the one approaching from the opposite direction.

Mental alertness is critical when driving on long stretches of rural road. With fewer vehicles and long distances between towns, it's easy to become drowsy or distracted. Staying focused, taking breaks when needed, and making sure you are well-rested before a long drive will help prevent fatigue-related accidents.

Every aspect of rural driving requires an extra level of caution and preparedness. The unpredictable nature of country roads means that even if you have driven the same route many times before, conditions can change without warning. By staying aware of potential hazards, adjusting your speed to match road conditions, and keeping safety as your top priority, you will be able to navigate Missouri's rural highways and backroads with confidence.

6.3 HIGHWAY AND INTERSTATE DRIVING

Missouri's highways and interstates provide the fastest and most efficient way to travel long distances, but they also require a different level of skill and awareness compared to driving on city streets or rural roads. Higher speeds, multiple lanes, heavy traffic, and complex interchanges demand that you remain focused and prepared for quick decision-making. Whether you are merging onto Interstate 70 in Kansas City, navigating the interchanges of Interstate 44 in St. Louis, or traveling along the rolling stretches of U.S. Route 60 in the southern part of the state, understanding the rules and best practices of highway and interstate driving is essential for your safety and the safety of others.

Merging onto a highway or interstate requires precision and confidence. Unlike local roads, where you may have more time to ease into traffic, highways move at higher speeds, and vehicles already on the road expect you to enter smoothly without disrupting the flow. Acceleration lanes, also known as *on-ramps*, are designed to give you the space needed to match the speed of traffic before merging. When entering, it is important to *signal early* to indicate your intention and check your mirrors and blind spots for an appropriate gap. If traffic is heavy, you may need to adjust your speed slightly, but stopping at the end of an acceleration lane should always be a last resort. The key is to merge smoothly without forcing other drivers to slow down or change lanes abruptly.

Lane discipline plays a crucial role in highway and interstate driving. Missouri follows the standard *keep right, pass left* rule, meaning that the right lanes are generally for slower-moving traffic, while the left lanes are used for passing. On highways with three or more lanes, the middle lane is often the best option for maintaining a steady speed, as the right lane is frequently used by vehicles merging or exiting, and the left lane should be kept clear for overtaking. Lingering in the left lane when not passing can create congestion and frustrate other drivers. If you are traveling at the speed limit but notice vehicles quickly approaching from behind, moving over to allow them to pass is the safest and most courteous action.

Speed limits on Missouri's interstates and highways vary depending on the area. The standard speed limit on most rural interstates is 70 mph, while urban interstates typically have lower limits, often around 60 mph or less. U.S. highways and state highways have more variation, with limits ranging from 55 to 65 mph depending on location and road conditions. It is crucial to pay attention to posted signs, as speed limits can change unexpectedly, especially near construction zones, curves, or heavily populated areas. Exceeding the speed limit not only increases the risk of losing control but also reduces the amount of time you have to react to sudden changes in traffic.

Maintaining a safe following distance is one of the most effective ways to prevent accidents on highways and interstates. At higher speeds, vehicles require a much greater stopping distance, meaning you need to leave enough space between your car and the one ahead. A good rule of thumb is the *three-second rule*—choosing a fixed object on the side of the road, such as a sign or a bridge, and ensuring that at least three seconds pass between the time the vehicle in front of you passes it and the time you reach the same point. In bad weather, such as heavy rain, fog, or ice, increasing this distance is necessary to compensate for reduced traction and visibility.

Passing other vehicles on a highway or interstate should always be done with caution. If you need to overtake a slower-moving vehicle, checking your mirrors and blind spots is essential before moving into the left lane. Signaling your intent and ensuring there is enough space to safely complete the pass without cutting too close to the other driver is equally important. Once you have passed, returning to the right lane is recommended unless you need to pass another vehicle. Passing on the right is generally discouraged unless traffic conditions make it unavoidable, such as when a slower vehicle remains in the left lane despite the right lane being open.

Interchanges and exits can be some of the most confusing parts of highway driving, especially in areas with complex systems of ramps and overpasses. Missouri's major cities, including St. Louis, Kansas City, and Springfield, have interchanges that may require you to merge, exit, or change lanes quickly. The best approach is to plan ahead by paying close attention to road signs and using navigation systems when necessary. Exits are usually marked well in advance, often with signs indicating the distance in miles before you need to exit. If you miss your exit, never stop or reverse on the highway—continue to the next available exit and find a safe way to get back on track.

Large commercial trucks are a common sight on Missouri's highways and interstates, and understanding how to drive safely around them is critical. Trucks have much larger blind spots than regular passenger vehicles, particularly on their right side and directly behind them. If you cannot see the truck driver in their side mirror, assume they cannot see you either. When passing a truck, always do so on the left side where the driver has a clearer view. Cutting in too closely in front of a truck is dangerous because these vehicles take much longer to stop than smaller cars. If a truck is merging onto the highway, giving them extra space rather than trying to speed past is the safer choice.

Construction zones are frequent along Missouri's highways, especially during the warmer months when roadwork is most active. These areas typically have reduced speed limits, narrow lanes, and potential lane closures. Ignoring reduced speed limits in work zones can result in hefty fines, as Missouri enforces strict penalties for speeding in these areas. Paying close attention to workers, temporary barriers, and changing road patterns is essential for keeping everyone safe.

Weather conditions can change quickly on Missouri's highways, creating additional hazards. Heavy rain can cause hydroplaning, where tires lose contact with the road surface and skid uncontrollably. If this happens, keeping a firm grip on the wheel and easing off the accelerator without braking suddenly can help regain control. Snow and ice create even more challenges, requiring reduced speeds, gentle braking, and careful steering. Fog, which is common in some areas during early morning hours, can significantly reduce visibility, making it important to use low-beam headlights and maintain extra following distance.

Fatigue is a serious concern for long-distance highway driving. Missouri's interstates can stretch for hundreds of miles, and the repetitive nature of driving at high speeds for long periods can lead to drowsiness. Taking breaks every two hours, drinking water, and stretching can help prevent fatigue. If you begin to feel tired, stopping at a rest area, gas station, or safe location to take a short break is the best decision.

Emergency situations on a highway or interstate require a calm and strategic response. If your vehicle breaks down, turning on your hazard lights and pulling off to the right shoulder as far as possible is the safest action. Exiting the vehicle should only be done if absolutely necessary, and standing too close to the roadway is extremely dangerous. If you have a flat tire or mechanical issue, calling for roadside assistance rather than attempting repairs on the shoulder is the safest option. In the event of an accident, remaining in your vehicle with your seatbelt fastened until emergency responders arrive is often the best course of action unless the situation presents an immediate danger.

Mastering highway and interstate driving in Missouri requires patience, attentiveness, and a solid understanding of traffic flow and road conditions. The ability to navigate interchanges smoothly, maintain safe speeds, and handle challenges such as construction, weather, and large trucks will make highway travel safer and more predictable. While high speeds and heavy traffic can seem intimidating at first, gaining experience and applying these best practices will give you the confidence to handle any highway or interstate with ease.

6.4 CONSTRUCTION ZONES AND WORK AREAS

Missouri's roads and highways are constantly undergoing maintenance, improvements, and expansions to keep them safe and efficient for drivers. This means you will frequently encounter *construction zones* and *work areas*, whether you are driving in a busy city, a quiet rural area, or on a high-speed interstate. These zones create unique challenges that require your full attention and understanding of the specific rules that apply. Reduced speed limits, unexpected lane shifts, temporary barriers, and the presence of workers make these areas more dangerous than normal roads. Being prepared to navigate them safely will not only keep you out of trouble but also help prevent accidents and delays.

One of the most important things to remember when approaching a construction zone is that *speed limits are always reduced*, and these limits are not optional. Missouri enforces strict penalties for speeding in work zones, with increased fines to discourage reckless driving. Even if workers are not visible at the moment, the lower speed limit still applies, as the road conditions may be altered due to loose gravel, narrow lanes, or construction equipment. Ignoring these speed reductions can result in not only a ticket but also a serious accident, as the normal road layout may be changed, requiring extra time to react to new conditions.

The presence of *work crews and equipment* makes these zones particularly dangerous. Construction workers are often close to moving traffic, relying on barriers, cones, and warning signs to keep them safe. However, their safety ultimately depends on how carefully you drive through the area. A moment of distraction, such as looking at your phone or adjusting the radio, can have devastating consequences if you fail to notice a worker stepping onto the road or a slow-moving construction vehicle ahead. In Missouri, hitting a worker in a construction zone carries severe legal consequences, including potential criminal charges, heavy fines, and loss of driving privileges.

Temporary *road signs and markings* in construction zones require your full attention. Standard lane markings may be replaced by temporary ones, which are sometimes faded or difficult to see, especially in bad weather. Bright orange signs warn you of upcoming changes, such as merging lanes, detours, or rough pavement. Flashing arrow boards may indicate which lanes are open or closed, and large digital signs often provide real-time information about upcoming traffic conditions. Paying attention to these signs and following their instructions will help you adjust your driving smoothly and avoid confusion.

Narrow lanes and shifting traffic patterns are common in work zones, making it essential to stay alert and in full control of your vehicle. When lanes are temporarily narrowed, there is less room for error, and drifting even slightly can put you dangerously close to barriers or other vehicles. Some construction projects involve lane shifts where the road curves unexpectedly or where traffic is directed onto a temporary path that may feel unfamiliar. Slowing down and keeping a steady hand on the wheel will help you maintain your lane position without sudden movements.

In many work zones, *lane closures* require you to merge into a single lane, often leading to congestion and frustration among drivers. The best approach is to merge early if possible, rather than waiting until the last second. However, in some cases, the *zipper merge* method is encouraged, where drivers take turns merging at the point where the lane ends. This technique is designed to keep traffic flowing smoothly and prevent long backups, but it only works if drivers cooperate and allow others to merge fairly. Aggressive driving or blocking other vehicles from merging only increases the risk of accidents and slows down traffic for everyone.

Another major challenge in construction zones is *uneven pavement and road debris*. Work areas often have rough patches, loose gravel, or raised surfaces where new asphalt meets old pavement. These conditions can make it harder to control your vehicle, especially at higher speeds. Driving over loose gravel can cause your tires to lose traction, increasing the risk of skidding. Raised pavement edges can create a sudden jolt, making it difficult to steer if you are not prepared. The best way to handle these hazards is to slow down, keep both hands on the wheel, and avoid sudden braking or sharp turns.

Construction vehicles and equipment often move slowly and may enter or exit the roadway unexpectedly. Large trucks carrying materials, bulldozers flattening gravel, or cement mixers pouring new pavement can block part of the road or create temporary obstacles. These vehicles typically have large blind spots, making it difficult for their operators to see smaller cars nearby. If you find yourself driving behind a construction vehicle, maintaining a safe following distance is crucial, as these vehicles may stop suddenly or kick up debris that could damage your windshield.

Nighttime construction work presents additional challenges due to reduced visibility and glare from bright work lights. Many road projects in Missouri are scheduled during the evening or early morning hours to minimize daytime traffic disruptions. While this can be convenient for regular commuters, it means you must be extra cautious when driving through these zones at night. Work lights can create harsh contrast, making it harder to see road markings, lane shifts, or workers on the road. Keeping your headlights on low beam and reducing your speed will help you adjust to the lighting conditions while staying aware of your surroundings.

When approaching a *flagger or traffic control worker*, it is critical to follow their directions without hesitation. These workers are there to guide traffic safely through the construction zone, often using stop/slow paddles or hand signals. Ignoring or misinterpreting their instructions can lead to confusion and dangerous situations. If a flagger signals you to stop, doing so promptly is essential, even if the road ahead appears clear. Construction vehicles or workers may be moving in an area not immediately visible to you, and waiting for their signal to proceed ensures that you do not put anyone at risk.

Heavy *traffic congestion* in work zones is common, particularly on busy highways and interstates. This often leads to sudden braking, frequent stops, and impatient drivers trying to weave through slow-moving lanes. Remaining calm and patient is key to avoiding accidents. Tailgating in a work zone is especially risky, as the vehicle in front of you may have to stop abruptly for a hazard or a worker on the road. Keeping a safe distance and anticipating slowdowns will help you avoid rear-end collisions.

If you miss an exit or a turn due to construction, never attempt to *reverse or make an illegal U-turn*. Work zones often have barriers and cones that make it difficult to turn around safely, and stopping in the middle of traffic to figure out where to go can create a dangerous situation. Instead, continue driving until you reach a safe place to exit or find an alternative route. Many construction zones have designated detours to help you navigate around road closures, and following these signs will guide you back on track without unnecessary risk.

When leaving a construction zone, it is important to *gradually return to normal speed* rather than accelerating too quickly. Many work areas have signs indicating when the reduced speed limit no longer applies, but rushing to reach full speed immediately can be dangerous, especially if traffic ahead is still adjusting to the change. Checking your mirrors and making sure the road is clear before increasing your speed will help ensure a smooth transition back to regular driving conditions.

Understanding how to navigate construction zones safely is not just about following the law—it is about protecting yourself, road workers, and other drivers. Every year, accidents in work areas result in injuries and fatalities that could have been prevented with greater attention and caution. By staying alert, reducing speed, and following posted signs and flagger instructions, you will contribute to a safer driving environment while also avoiding fines and unnecessary delays. Developing the habit of driving carefully through work zones will prepare you for handling these situations confidently, no matter where your journey takes you.

CHAPTER 7
SPECIAL DRIVING SITUATIONS

7.1 NIGHT DRIVING: VISIBILITY AND SAFETY TIPS

Driving at night presents unique challenges that require heightened attention, careful adjustments, and a solid understanding of how reduced visibility affects road safety. In Missouri, where rural highways, suburban roads, and city streets all pose different nighttime hazards, knowing how to adapt your driving in the dark is crucial. The absence of natural daylight makes it harder to see obstacles, judge distances, and react quickly to sudden changes in traffic conditions. Streetlights may provide some illumination in urban areas, but rural roads can be pitch black, with only your headlights guiding the way. Wildlife, impaired drivers, and fatigued motorists further contribute to the risks, making it essential to take every precaution to stay safe.

Your *headlights* are your most valuable tool when driving after dark. Missouri law requires you to turn them on from 30 minutes after sunset until 30 minutes before sunrise, but relying on them sooner rather than later can help you see more clearly and ensure other drivers notice you. Even during twilight hours, when the sky still holds some light, shadows can obscure pedestrians, cyclists, or animals darting across the road. Keeping your headlights on not only helps you see better but also increases your visibility to others. However, proper use of headlights goes beyond just turning them on. The high beam setting provides a stronger, longer-reaching light, but using it improperly can be dangerous. If you are on a road with oncoming traffic, it is essential to switch to low beams to avoid blinding other drivers. Similarly, when following another vehicle, keeping your headlights on low beam prevents the glare from reflecting in their mirrors, which can be distracting or even hazardous.

One of the most underestimated dangers of night driving is *glare*. The bright lights from streetlamps, neon signs, and headlights of other vehicles can create a harsh contrast against the dark surroundings, making it difficult for your eyes to adjust. If an approaching car has its high beams on, looking slightly to the right at the edge of your lane can help you avoid the full effect of the glare while still keeping the road in view. Additionally, keeping your windshield clean, both inside and out, can prevent light from scattering and causing further visual distortion. Smudges, dirt, or streaks may not seem significant during the day, but at night, they can catch light in a way that reduces clarity and makes it harder to see obstacles.

Reduced visibility means that your *reaction time* must be sharper. At night, objects in the distance appear much later than they do during daylight, giving you less time to respond to sudden changes in traffic, road conditions, or unexpected hazards. Because of this, increasing your *following distance* is essential. While the standard safe distance during the day is about three seconds between your car and the vehicle in front of you, extending this to at least four or five seconds at night gives you a greater buffer to react if the driver ahead suddenly brakes or swerves. This is especially important on highways, where speeds are higher, and a delayed reaction can lead to serious consequences.

Certain roads in Missouri are known for *wildlife crossings*, and nighttime is when animals are most active. Deer, raccoons, and even larger animals like elk in the southern parts of the state can suddenly appear in your path, creating a serious collision risk. If you see a deer on the side of the road, it is important to slow down immediately, as deer often travel in groups. If one has crossed, there is a high chance that others will follow. Flashing your high beams may sometimes help scare animals away, but if a deer is already in the road, honking your horn and braking firmly (without swerving) is the safest way to avoid an accident.

Fatigue is another major risk when driving at night. Many people underestimate how quickly *drowsiness* can impair judgment, slow reaction time, and reduce awareness. The body's natural rhythm makes late-night driving especially difficult, as energy levels decrease, and the brain becomes less alert. If you start to feel heavy-eyed, yawn excessively, or have trouble keeping your focus, it is best to pull over in a safe location and take a short break. Rolling down the windows for fresh air or turning up the radio may provide a temporary boost, but they are not reliable solutions. If you are truly fatigued, stopping to rest is the only way to ensure you are driving safely.

In urban areas, nighttime brings *different challenges*, including the increased presence of pedestrians, cyclists, and unpredictable drivers. City streets may be well-lit, but distractions such as flashing advertisements, crowded intersections, and nightlife activity can make it difficult to notice smaller hazards. People leaving bars or nightclubs may not be fully aware of their surroundings, and some may step into the road unexpectedly. Keeping an eye on crosswalks, scanning the sidewalks for movement, and driving at a controlled speed will help you anticipate and react to these situations before they become dangerous.

Parking lots and driveways are especially risky at night because of limited visibility and unexpected movements from other vehicles or pedestrians. When pulling out of a parking space, double-checking blind spots and backing up slowly will reduce the chance of hitting an unseen pedestrian or car. Many newer vehicles are equipped with backup cameras and sensors, but relying solely on technology can create a false sense of security. Physically turning your head to check for obstacles remains the best way to ensure a clear path.

Weather conditions can further complicate nighttime driving. Rain, fog, or snow significantly reduce visibility and make roads more slippery. In foggy conditions, using your high beams is actually counterproductive, as the light reflects off the moisture in the air, creating a white wall effect. Instead, low beams or fog lights should be used to help you see without excessive glare. If roads are wet or icy, slowing down and maintaining steady, controlled movements will help prevent skidding.

Proper maintenance of your vehicle plays a significant role in safe nighttime driving. Dirty or misaligned headlights can reduce visibility, making it harder to see the road ahead. Regularly cleaning your headlights and checking their alignment ensures that they provide maximum illumination. Additionally, making sure your *taillights and brake lights* are functioning correctly is essential for allowing other drivers to see you. A burned-out brake light may not seem like a major issue, but it can make it harder for the driver behind you to recognize when you are stopping, increasing the risk of a rear-end collision.

Road construction often takes place at night to avoid daytime traffic congestion. Work zones can be more difficult to navigate in the dark, especially if lane markings are temporarily changed or construction vehicles are entering and exiting the roadway. Paying close attention to warning signs, reducing speed, and watching for workers near the road will help you get through these areas safely.

Another major factor to be aware of is the presence of *impaired drivers*. While impaired driving is illegal at any time of day, it becomes more common at night, particularly on weekends and holidays. Drivers under the influence of alcohol or drugs often exhibit erratic behavior, such as drifting between lanes, sudden braking, or inconsistent speeds. If you notice a vehicle driving unpredictably, keeping your distance and reporting them to the authorities if necessary can prevent accidents.

Missouri law enforcement regularly conducts *sobriety checkpoints* and increased nighttime patrols to deter impaired driving. If you are stopped at a checkpoint, following instructions calmly and providing your license and registration when requested will help the process go smoothly. Officers conduct these checks to ensure road safety, and cooperating respectfully will allow you to continue your journey without issue.

Driving at night requires a combination of heightened awareness, patience, and the ability to adapt to changing conditions. The dark environment reduces visibility, making it crucial to rely on your headlights, increase following distances, and stay vigilant for obstacles. Hazards such as wildlife, impaired drivers, and unpredictable pedestrians make nighttime travel more dangerous than daytime driving, but by practicing safe habits and staying alert, you can navigate Missouri's roads confidently, no matter the hour.

7.2 DRIVING IN ADVERSE WEATHER CONDITIONS

Missouri experiences a wide range of weather conditions throughout the year, and knowing how to handle your vehicle in different types of adverse weather is crucial for staying safe on the road. Whether you encounter heavy rain, dense fog, ice, snow, or strong winds, each presents unique challenges that can make driving more dangerous. Road conditions can change rapidly, sometimes within minutes, making it important to anticipate potential hazards and adjust your driving habits accordingly. Poor visibility, reduced traction, and unpredictable movements from other drivers mean that you have to be extra cautious and ready to react to sudden changes.

Rain is one of the most common weather conditions that affects driving in Missouri. Light rain may not seem like a big issue, but the first few minutes of rainfall can be the most dangerous. When water mixes with oil, dirt, and other debris on the road, it creates a slick surface that reduces tire grip, increasing the likelihood of skidding. This is especially true in urban areas with high traffic, where oil from vehicles builds up on the pavement. You should always reduce your speed when it starts raining and give yourself extra time to stop. Braking suddenly on wet roads can cause your tires to lose traction, leading to hydroplaning—a situation where your car slides uncontrollably over the water. If this happens, taking your foot off the gas and steering in the direction you want to go while avoiding sudden movements can help you regain control. Keeping your windshield wipers in good condition and using your defroster when necessary will ensure you have a clear view of the road.

Fog is another common hazard, particularly in the early morning and late at night. Dense fog can reduce visibility to just a few feet, making it nearly impossible to see road signs, traffic lights, or other vehicles. If you ever find yourself driving in heavy fog, using your *low beam headlights* is essential. High beams can actually make visibility worse by reflecting off the fog and creating a bright white glare that further obscures the road. If the fog is thick enough that you can barely see in front of you, slowing down significantly and keeping a safe distance from the vehicle ahead will give you more time to react if traffic suddenly stops. In extreme conditions, it may be safest to pull over at a well-lit area or rest stop and wait for the fog to lift.

Snow and ice present some of the most dangerous driving conditions, particularly in the winter months when Missouri experiences cold snaps and unpredictable storms. Ice is especially hazardous because it can be nearly invisible, appearing as a thin layer on bridges, overpasses, and shaded areas of the road. Black ice, in particular, is one of the most deceptive dangers—it forms when moisture on the pavement freezes into a clear, smooth layer that looks just like wet asphalt. Since you cannot always see ice before driving over it, staying aware of temperature changes and paying attention to road surface textures can help you anticipate where it might be. If your car begins to slide on ice, the most important thing to remember is to *stay calm*. Sudden braking or jerking the steering wheel can make the skid worse. Instead, easing off the accelerator and gently turning in the direction of the skid will help you regain control.

Before heading out in snowy or icy conditions, making sure your car is properly equipped can prevent a dangerous situation. Using *winter tires* can significantly improve your traction, as they are designed to grip icy roads better than regular tires. Keeping your gas tank at least half full can also prevent your fuel line from freezing, a problem that can leave you stranded in freezing temperatures. Visibility is another major concern in the winter, so always clear your windshield, windows, and mirrors of snow and ice before driving. Relying on your defroster and wipers alone is not enough—any remaining ice on your car can obstruct your vision or fly off while driving, creating hazards for others.

Heavy winds can be just as dangerous as other forms of extreme weather, especially on highways and open roads where gusts can push your vehicle sideways or cause sudden shifts in steering. Strong winds are particularly risky for *high-profile vehicles* like trucks, SUVs, and vans, which have larger surfaces that catch the wind more easily. If you feel your car being pushed to one side, keeping a firm grip on the steering wheel and making small, steady corrections will help you stay in your lane. When passing large trucks or driving near open fields, expect sudden gusts and be prepared to counteract them. Windy conditions also increase the risk of debris on the road, such as fallen branches, trash, or even road signs that have been knocked over. Staying alert and scanning ahead will help you spot these obstacles before they become a problem.

Thunderstorms bring a combination of hazards, including heavy rain, lightning, and strong winds. In Missouri, severe thunderstorms can develop quickly, producing conditions that make driving extremely dangerous. If a storm is approaching and the rain becomes too intense to see properly, pulling over in a safe location away from trees and power lines is the safest option. Never attempt to drive through flooded roads, even if the water appears shallow. It only takes a few inches of water to cause your car to lose traction, and deeper water can stall your engine or even carry your vehicle away in a strong current. Flash flooding can occur with little warning, especially in low-lying areas, so always pay attention to weather alerts and avoid driving during heavy storms whenever possible.

Tornadoes are another severe weather threat in Missouri, especially in the spring and summer months when warm and cold air masses collide. If you are driving and receive a tornado warning, looking for immediate shelter is the best course of action. Overpasses may seem like safe places to take cover, but the wind can actually intensify in these areas, making them dangerous. Instead, if no safe building is nearby, staying in your car, keeping your seatbelt fastened, and covering your head with your hands or a thick blanket can help protect you from flying debris.

When driving in extreme weather conditions, maintaining a cautious mindset is the key to staying safe. Slowing down, increasing your following distance, and adjusting your driving habits to match the conditions can make a significant difference in preventing accidents. Paying attention to weather forecasts before heading out and keeping emergency supplies in your vehicle—such as a flashlight, blanket, water, and a basic first-aid kit—can prepare you for unexpected delays or dangerous situations. Missouri's weather can change rapidly, but knowing how to handle your vehicle in rain, fog, snow, wind, and storms will help you stay in control and navigate the roads safely, no matter what conditions you encounter.

7.3 MOUNTAIN AND HILL DRIVING CONSIDERATIONS

Missouri may not have the towering peaks found in states like Colorado or Montana, but the Ozark Mountains and the rolling hills of the state present their own unique challenges when driving. Elevation changes, steep inclines, winding roads, and unpredictable weather patterns can all make hill and mountain driving more complex than cruising along flat highways. Adjusting your driving techniques to suit these conditions is essential for maintaining control of your vehicle and ensuring your safety on the road.

When approaching an incline, understanding how to manage your speed and power is crucial. If you apply too much acceleration too quickly, your tires can lose traction, especially on wet or icy roads. On the other hand, failing to give your vehicle enough power can result in losing momentum before reaching the top of the hill, which can be especially dangerous on two-lane roads where passing opportunities are limited. A steady, controlled increase in speed before reaching the base of the hill allows you to use the natural momentum of your vehicle to climb efficiently. If you are driving a car with a manual transmission, shifting to a lower gear will give you more power and prevent excessive strain on the engine.

Descending a hill or mountain requires just as much care, if not more, than climbing. Gravity increases your speed as you go downhill, and if you rely too much on your brakes, they can overheat and lose effectiveness. Instead of holding your foot on the brake pedal for the entire descent, shifting into a lower gear helps your engine slow the car naturally, reducing the strain on your brakes. This technique, called *engine braking*, is commonly used by truck drivers on steep declines to prevent brake failure. If you ever notice a burning smell while going downhill, it could be a sign that your brakes are overheating, which means you should find a safe place to pull over and let them cool before continuing.

Curves and switchbacks are another common feature of hill and mountain roads, particularly in the Ozarks, where winding routes follow the natural contours of the land. Sharp turns limit your visibility and require precise control to navigate safely. Before entering a curve, reducing your speed is essential, as braking while turning can cause your tires to lose traction, especially in wet or icy conditions. Staying in your lane and avoiding cutting corners is critical, as oncoming traffic may be approaching around a blind curve. Many roads in hilly regions lack wide shoulders, meaning there is little room for error if you drift too far to the side.

Another factor to consider when driving in the hills and mountains of Missouri is the potential for wildlife crossings. Forested areas and remote roads often mean deer, raccoons, or even wild turkeys can suddenly appear in your path. Collisions with large animals, particularly deer, can cause serious damage to your vehicle and injuries to both you and the animal. Staying alert and scanning ahead, especially at dawn and dusk when wildlife is most active, can help you spot movement on the roadside before an animal darts into the road. If you see one deer, assume there may be more nearby, as they often travel in groups.

Weather conditions in Missouri's hilly regions can also change rapidly, especially during colder months. Fog can settle into valleys and lower elevations, reducing visibility, while sudden rain showers can make roads slippery. In winter, icy patches are common on shaded areas of the road, even when the sun has melted snow and ice elsewhere. Bridges and overpasses freeze more quickly than the rest of the road because cold air circulates above and below them, so extra caution is needed when crossing them. If you ever find yourself driving on a steep hill covered in ice or snow, making gentle movements and avoiding sudden acceleration or braking will help prevent your car from sliding. Carrying emergency supplies, such as a flashlight, blankets, and a small shovel, can be a lifesaver if road conditions become too hazardous to continue.

Another important aspect of driving in hilly areas is being aware of the potential for falling rocks and road debris. In some areas, especially after heavy rain, rocks can loosen from slopes and roll onto the roadway, creating sudden obstacles. Signs indicating *Falling Rock Zones* are common in parts of the state where landslides or rockslides can occur. Keeping your eyes on the road ahead and avoiding distractions will allow you to react quickly if an object appears in your path.

If you find yourself behind a slow-moving vehicle, such as a large truck or a car towing a trailer, patience is key. Many hilly roads in Missouri have designated *passing zones* where you can safely overtake slower traffic, but doing so requires careful judgment. Never attempt to pass on a curve or a hill where you cannot see what is ahead. If you are the slower-moving vehicle, using a pull-off area or letting faster traffic pass when it is safe can help maintain a smooth flow of vehicles on winding roads.

Missouri's hills and mountains offer some of the most scenic and enjoyable driving experiences in the state, but they also require extra awareness and skill. Whether you are navigating steep inclines, sharp curves, or unexpected wildlife crossings, staying prepared and adapting your driving techniques to the terrain will help you stay safe and in control.

7.4 NAVIGATING MISSOURI'S ROUNDABOUTS AND TRAFFIC CIRCLES

Roundabouts and traffic circles are becoming more common across Missouri, and understanding how to navigate them properly is essential for smooth and safe driving. Unlike traditional intersections controlled by traffic lights or stop signs, roundabouts keep traffic flowing continuously, reducing congestion and lowering the likelihood of severe accidents. Because vehicles are always moving in the same direction around a central island, the risk of head-on or high-speed T-bone collisions is significantly reduced. However, if you are unfamiliar with these circular intersections, they can seem confusing at first. Knowing when to enter, when to yield, and how to exit correctly will make your experience much easier and safer.

Before reaching a roundabout, paying attention to road signs and lane markings is key to understanding your path. A roundabout typically has *advance warning signs* that indicate its presence ahead, along with arrows showing the direction of travel. These signs help you prepare by selecting the correct lane before you enter. Many multi-lane roundabouts have pavement markings and overhead signs that indicate which lane to use for your intended destination. If you need to turn right, you should be in the rightmost lane. If you plan to go straight or take the second exit, you may need to stay in the middle lane. For left turns or U-turns, the left lane is usually required. Staying in the correct lane before entering prevents last-second lane changes, which can lead to confusion and crashes.

As you approach the roundabout, the most important rule to remember is that *traffic already inside the roundabout always has the right of way.* You must slow down and yield to any vehicles coming from the left. If there are no cars inside, or if there is a safe gap, you can proceed without stopping. Unlike a four-way stop, you do not need to come to a complete halt unless traffic is heavy. Entering smoothly without stopping unnecessarily helps maintain the continuous flow that makes roundabouts so effective at reducing congestion.

Once inside, maintaining a steady speed and following the curve of the road is crucial. There is no need to rush or stop inside the roundabout. Sudden braking can cause rear-end collisions, as drivers behind you may not expect an abrupt stop in a moving intersection. Looking ahead and keeping a safe following distance will give you enough reaction time if another vehicle suddenly slows down. You should also avoid cutting across lanes or making sharp, last-minute turns. If you accidentally enter the wrong lane or miss your exit, continue around the roundabout until you can safely exit in the correct direction.

Exiting a roundabout is just as important as entering it correctly. As you approach your desired exit, using your *right turn signal* lets other drivers know that you are leaving. This small but crucial step prevents confusion for those behind you and reduces the risk of last-minute swerving. Checking your blind spots is also important, as cyclists or pedestrians may be crossing at designated crosswalks near the exits. Many roundabouts are designed with pedestrian safety in mind, with marked crossings set slightly away from the actual intersection to allow drivers more time to react.

Missouri has been expanding the use of roundabouts in both urban and rural areas due to their benefits in reducing traffic delays and improving safety. Studies have shown that roundabouts lead to fewer severe crashes compared to traditional intersections. While minor fender-benders can still occur if drivers fail to yield or misjudge spacing, the circular design naturally slows vehicles down, making high-speed collisions unlikely. Because roundabouts do not rely on traffic signals, they also continue to function smoothly during power outages, unlike stoplights that require electricity to operate.

One variation of a roundabout you may encounter is a *mini-roundabout*, often found in residential neighborhoods or low-traffic areas. These are smaller in size and sometimes have a raised painted circle in the middle rather than a full landscaped island. The same rules apply—vehicles must yield to traffic inside and travel in a counterclockwise direction—but the compact design makes them easier to navigate at lower speeds.

Another version is a *multi-lane roundabout*, which requires extra attention to lane positioning. Unlike single-lane roundabouts, where all vehicles travel in one shared lane, multi-lane roundabouts have separate lanes that guide traffic toward different exits. It is important to select your lane before entering, as changing lanes inside the roundabout can be dangerous. If lane markings are present, following them carefully ensures you stay in the correct path for your intended exit.

For larger vehicles, such as trucks or buses, navigating a roundabout requires slightly different handling. Many roundabouts have an *apron*, which is a slightly raised, paved area around the center island. This design allows oversized vehicles to safely maneuver through the intersection without crossing into other lanes. If you are driving behind a truck, giving it extra space is necessary, as its turning radius will be wider than that of a standard car. Large vehicles may also need to use both lanes to complete a turn, so avoiding driving alongside them in a roundabout is the safest approach.

In some cases, you may encounter a *double roundabout*, also known as a *dogbone* or *dumbbell* roundabout. These are often used near highway interchanges or in areas where two roundabouts are placed close together to manage traffic flow efficiently. The key to navigating these is to treat each one as a separate intersection, following the same yield and exit rules as with a standard roundabout.

Understanding how to drive through roundabouts properly not only helps you move through traffic more efficiently but also enhances overall road safety. Whether you are traveling through a single-lane neighborhood roundabout or a multi-lane version on a busy highway, keeping a steady pace, yielding to vehicles already inside, signaling your exits, and staying aware of pedestrians will ensure that you handle these intersections with confidence.

The Missouri Drivers Permit Study Book 2025

CHAPTER 8
PRACTICE TESTS AND STUDY RESOURCES

8.1 PRACTICE TEST 1

(25 multiple-choice questions, passing score: 80% or at least 20 correct answers)

Instructions:
- Read each question carefully and select the **best** answer.
- There is only **one correct answer** for each question.
- Take your time, but try to answer as if you were taking the real test.

1. What does a yellow diamond-shaped road sign indicate?
A) A regulatory law that must be followed
B) A warning about upcoming road conditions or hazards
C) A direction that must be followed
D) A speed limit change ahead

2. When approaching a stop sign, what must you do?
A) Slow down and proceed if no other vehicles are coming
B) Stop only if there is cross traffic
C) Come to a complete stop before the crosswalk, stop line, or intersection
D) Honk your horn before stopping

3. What is the legal speed limit on rural highways in Missouri, unless otherwise posted?
A) 55 mph
B) 65 mph
C) 70 mph
D) 50 mph

4. If a traffic signal light is not working, what should you do?
A) Treat it as if it were a four-way stop sign
B) Drive through with caution
C) Ignore it if there is no police officer directing traffic
D) Speed up to avoid confusion

5. What should you do if an emergency vehicle with flashing lights is approaching you from behind?
A) Speed up to get out of the way
B) Move to the right side of the road and stop
C) Stop immediately in your lane
D) Ignore it unless the siren is on

6. A solid yellow line on your side of the centerline means:

A) You may pass at any time
B) Passing is allowed if the road is clear
C) Passing is not allowed
D) You must turn left at the next intersection

7. When are you required to use your headlights in Missouri?
A) Only when driving in rural areas
B) Between sunset and sunrise or during poor visibility conditions
C) Only when there is fog
D) Only when other drivers flash their headlights at you

8. If you are driving on a highway and miss your exit, what should you do?
A) Stop and back up carefully
B) Make a U-turn at the nearest intersection
C) Continue driving to the next exit
D) Pull over and ask for directions

9. What does a flashing red traffic light mean?
A) Slow down and proceed with caution
B) Stop completely, then proceed when safe
C) Stop only if there is traffic
D) The traffic signal is out of order

10. What should you do if you are involved in a minor accident with no injuries?
A) Call the police immediately and remain in your vehicle
B) Move your vehicle out of traffic, exchange information, and report it if required
C) Leave the scene if the damage is minor
D) Continue driving without stopping if the other driver waves you on

11. What is the legal blood alcohol concentration (BAC) limit for drivers 21 and older in Missouri?
A) 0.08%
B) 0.05%
C) 0.02%
D) 0.10%

12. If you are being tailgated, what should you do?
A) Slow down gradually to encourage the driver to pass
B) Slam on your brakes
C) Speed up to create more space
D) Make an abrupt turn to get out of the way

13. A school bus with flashing red lights has stopped ahead. What should you do?
A) Slow down and pass cautiously
B) Stop regardless of which direction you are coming from
C) Stop only if children are crossing the road
D) Honk to alert the children you are passing

14. When making a left turn at an intersection, you should:
A) Yield to oncoming traffic and pedestrians
B) Always turn before oncoming traffic reaches the intersection
C) Speed up to clear the intersection quickly
D) Ignore pedestrians since they must yield to vehicles

15. What is the proper hand signal for a left turn?
A) Left arm extended straight out
B) Left arm bent upward at a 90-degree angle
C) Left arm bent downward at a 90-degree angle
D) Right arm extended straight out

16. If your vehicle begins to skid, what should you do?
A) Slam on the brakes
B) Steer in the direction of the skid
C) Turn the wheel sharply in the opposite direction of the skid
D) Accelerate to regain control

17. What should you do when driving in heavy rain and your vehicle starts to hydroplane?
A) Apply the brakes firmly
B) Steer sharply to correct your direction
C) Take your foot off the gas and steer straight
D) Speed up to drive through the water

18. Missouri's "Move Over" law requires drivers to:
A) Move to the right lane whenever another vehicle is passing
B) Change lanes or slow down when approaching emergency vehicles on the roadside
C) Stop completely if an emergency vehicle is parked ahead
D) Yield to police officers only if they have their sirens on

19. When parallel parking, your vehicle should be within how many inches of the curb?
A) 18 inches
B) 12 inches
C) 6 inches
D) 24 inches

20. A yellow light means:
A) Stop immediately
B) Speed up to beat the red light
C) Slow down and prepare to stop if safe
D) The light is malfunctioning

21. If you see a pedestrian with a white cane, you should assume that the person is:
A) A construction worker
B) Visually impaired
C) A traffic officer
D) A jogger

22. A broken white line on the road means:
A) Passing is not allowed
B) Lanes are moving in opposite directions
C) You may change lanes if it is safe
D) You must stay in your lane at all times

23. What is the penalty for driving without auto insurance in Missouri?
A) A fine and possible license suspension
B) Only a warning
C) A two-week driving suspension
D) No penalty

24. If an intersection has no stop signs or traffic signals, who has the right of way?
A) The driver on the left
B) The driver who reaches the intersection first
C) The driver on the right
D) The larger vehicle

25. What is the safest way to drive in a work zone?
A) Follow posted speed limits and watch for workers
B) Speed up to avoid delays
C) Drive in the middle of the road
D) Ignore signs if no workers are present

Answer Key & Explanations
1. B) Warning signs are yellow and diamond-shaped.
2. C) You must come to a complete stop before proceeding.
3. B) The default speed limit on rural highways in Missouri is 65 mph.
4. A) Treat a non-functioning traffic light as a four-way stop.
5. B) Pull over to the right and stop.
6. C) A solid yellow line means no passing.

The Missouri Drivers Permit Study Book 2025

7. B) Headlights must be used between sunset and sunrise or when visibility is poor.
8. C) Never reverse; take the next exit.
9. B) A flashing red light functions like a stop sign.
10. B) Move out of traffic and exchange details.
11. A) 0.08% is the legal BAC limit.
12. A) Slowing down can encourage the tailgater to pass.
13. B) You must stop for a school bus with flashing red lights.
14. A) Always yield when making a left turn.
15. A) The correct signal for a left turn is a straight-out arm.
16. B) Steer in the direction of the skid.
17. C) Ease off the gas and steer straight.
18. B) Slow down or change lanes for emergency vehicles.
19. A) You must be within 18 inches of the curb.
20. C) Yellow means slow down and prepare to stop.
21. B) A white cane indicates visual impairment.
22. C) A broken white line allows lane changes.
23. A) Driving uninsured can result in fines and suspension.
24. C) The driver on the right has the right of way.
25. A) Follow speed limits and be alert.

The Missouri Drivers Permit Study Book 2025

8.2 PRACTICE TEST 2

(25 multiple-choice questions, passing score: 80% or at least 20 correct answers)

Instructions:
- Read each question carefully and choose the **best** answer.
- There is only **one correct answer** for each question.
- Answer as if you were taking the real test.

1. What is the primary purpose of Missouri's Graduated Driver Licensing (GDL) program?
A) To allow new drivers to drive without restrictions
B) To gradually introduce young drivers to safe driving practices
C) To limit the number of people who can obtain a driver's license
D) To prevent anyone under 18 from driving

2. A flashing yellow light at an intersection means:
A) Stop and wait for a green light
B) Slow down and proceed with caution
C) The traffic signal is broken
D) Only turn left if the way is clear

3. If you are driving in Missouri and an officer signals for you to pull over, what should you do?
A) Speed up to find a safer place to stop
B) Pull over to the right side of the road as soon as it is safe
C) Ignore the officer if you did nothing wrong
D) Stop immediately in the middle of the road

4. What is the minimum following distance you should maintain behind another vehicle in normal driving conditions?
A) One car length
B) Two seconds
C) Three to four seconds
D) Ten feet

5. What should you do if you see a railroad crossing sign ahead?
A) Slow down and be prepared to stop if necessary
B) Speed up to cross quickly
C) Stop immediately
D) Ignore it unless you see a train

6. When should you yield the right of way to pedestrians?
A) Only when they are in a crosswalk
B) Only when they have a "Walk" signal

The Missouri Drivers Permit Study Book 2025
C) Always, whether they are in a crosswalk or not
D) Never, since vehicles have the right of way

7. What should you do if your brakes fail while driving?
A) Pump the brakes and downshift to a lower gear
B) Honk your horn and turn off the ignition
C) Accelerate to find a safe spot to stop
D) Close your eyes and brace for impact

8. If you are driving on a divided highway and see a school bus with flashing red lights on the opposite side, what should you do?
A) Stop immediately
B) Slow down but keep driving
C) Stop only if there is no physical barrier between you and the bus
D) Ignore the bus unless children are crossing

9. If your vehicle starts to drift off the pavement, what should you do?
A) Steer sharply back onto the road
B) Hold the wheel firmly, slow down, and gently steer back onto the road
C) Slam on the brakes
D) Accelerate to regain control

10. When turning right at an intersection, which lane should you turn into?
A) The farthest left lane
B) Any lane that is open
C) The right lane, closest to the curb
D) The middle lane

11. What should you do if you are driving at night and an oncoming vehicle has its high beams on?
A) Flash your headlights quickly to signal them
B) Look directly into the bright lights
C) Slow down and turn on your high beams
D) Look slightly to the right side of the road to avoid glare

12. What is the penalty for failing to stop for a school bus with its stop arm extended in Missouri?
A) A warning
B) A fine and possible license suspension
C) A ticket but no points on your license
D) No penalty if no children were harmed

13. When can you legally pass another vehicle on the right?
A) When the other vehicle is turning left, and there is room to pass safely
B) On any two-lane road

C) When driving in a school zone
D) Only on highways

14. If two vehicles arrive at an intersection with stop signs at the same time, who has the right of way?
A) The larger vehicle
B) The driver on the left
C) The driver on the right
D) The vehicle going straight

15. What is the purpose of a roundabout?
A) To slow down traffic and improve flow
B) To confuse drivers
C) To allow U-turns in residential areas
D) To replace all traffic signals

16. What should you do if you need to turn but there is a bicyclist in the bike lane?
A) Turn quickly before the cyclist gets there
B) Honk to make the cyclist stop
C) Yield to the cyclist before turning
D) Block the bike lane while waiting to turn

17. If your car begins to overheat, what should you do?
A) Keep driving until you reach your destination
B) Turn off the air conditioning and pull over safely
C) Open the radiator cap immediately
D) Speed up to cool the engine

18. What is the best way to avoid distractions while driving?
A) Keep the radio at full volume
B) Use your phone only at stoplights
C) Focus on the road and avoid activities like texting or eating
D) Only drive in low-traffic areas

19. When backing out of a parking space, what is the safest method?
A) Check mirrors and back up quickly
B) Look over your shoulder and proceed slowly
C) Rely on your backup camera only
D) Honk to warn others before moving

20. What does a green arrow mean at a traffic light?
A) Stop
B) Turn in the direction of the arrow if the way is clear
C) Slow down and yield
D) Proceed straight only

21. If your vehicle has an anti-lock braking system (ABS), what should you do in an emergency stop?
A) Pump the brakes
B) Press and hold the brake pedal firmly
C) Release the brakes and steer
D) Turn off the engine

22. If you are involved in a serious accident, what is the first thing you should do?
A) Call for emergency assistance
B) Move your vehicle immediately
C) Leave the scene if you are unharmed
D) Argue with the other driver

23. What is Missouri's "Implied Consent Law"?
A) It allows police to stop any driver at any time
B) It means you automatically agree to a breathalyzer test when driving
C) It requires drivers to give pedestrians the right of way
D) It allows minors to drive with a permit

24. If you are driving in fog, what should you do?
A) Use high beams to see better
B) Turn on your hazard lights
C) Use low-beam headlights and drive cautiously
D) Speed up to clear the fog faster

25. What should you do if your vehicle stalls on railroad tracks and a train is approaching?
A) Stay inside and try to restart the car
B) Exit the vehicle and run away at an angle toward the train
C) Push the car off the tracks
D) Call the police and stay with the vehicle

Answer Key & Explanations
1. B) The GDL program helps new drivers gain experience.
2. B) A flashing yellow light means proceed with caution.
3. B) Always pull over safely when signaled by an officer.
4. C) Maintain a 3-4 second following distance.
5. A) Be ready to stop at railroad crossings.
6. C) Always yield to pedestrians.
7. A) Pump brakes and shift to a lower gear.
8. C) Stop if there is no median.
9. B) Slow down and ease back onto the road.
10. C) Turn into the right lane.
11. D) Look slightly to the right to avoid glare.

12. B) Failing to stop for a school bus can lead to fines.
13. A) You may pass on the right if the other vehicle is turning left.
14. C) The driver on the right has the right of way.
15. A) Roundabouts improve traffic flow.
16. C) Always yield to bicyclists.
17. B) Turn off A/C and pull over safely.
18. C) Avoid distractions by focusing on the road.
19. B) Look over your shoulder and back up slowly.
20. B) A green arrow means you can turn if clear.
21. B) ABS requires firm, steady braking.
22. A) Call emergency services immediately.
23. B) Implied Consent Law requires drivers to submit to alcohol tests.
24. C) Use low beams and drive cautiously.
25. B) Run away at an angle toward the train.

8.3 PRACTICE TEST 3

(25 multiple-choice questions, passing score: 80% or at least 20 correct answers)

Instructions:
- Read each question carefully and choose the **best** answer.
- There is only **one correct answer** for each question.
- Answer as if you were taking the real test.

1. What should you do when approaching an intersection with a non-functioning traffic signal?
A) Treat it like a four-way stop
B) Proceed through at normal speed
C) Only stop if other cars are present
D) Speed up to avoid confusion

2. When parking uphill with a curb, which way should you turn your front wheels?
A) Toward the curb
B) Away from the curb
C) Keep them straight
D) It doesn't matter

3. If you are driving and need to use your windshield wipers due to rain, what else should you do?
A) Turn on your hazard lights
B) Slow down to 10 mph
C) Turn on your headlights
D) Stop driving immediately

4. If an emergency vehicle is approaching with lights and sirens on, what must you do?
A) Speed up to stay ahead of it
B) Move as far to the right as possible and stop
C) Maintain your speed and direction
D) Stop only if the emergency vehicle is behind you

5. What does a double solid yellow line on the road indicate?
A) You may pass if traffic is clear
B) Passing is not allowed in either direction
C) You can pass only on the left
D) It is a pedestrian crossing area

6. When driving on a wet road, what is the greatest risk?
A) Your tires may wear down faster
B) You may experience hydroplaning

C) The road will become less visible
D) Your windshield may fog up

7. What does a flashing red light at an intersection mean?
A) Proceed without stopping
B) Stop completely, then proceed when safe
C) Slow down and be cautious
D) Ignore it if no other cars are around

8. What is the best way to handle a skid?
A) Slam on the brakes
B) Steer in the direction you want to go
C) Steer in the opposite direction of the skid
D) Accelerate to regain traction

9. What is the Missouri "Move Over" law?
A) You must change lanes or slow down for stopped emergency vehicles
B) You must move out of the way of aggressive drivers
C) You must always drive in the right lane
D) You must move over when being tailgated

10. If you miss your exit on the highway, what should you do?
A) Stop and back up
B) Continue to the next exit
C) Make a U-turn
D) Pull over and wait for traffic to clear

11. When are you required to use your turn signal?
A) Only when making left turns
B) At least 100 feet before a turn or lane change
C) Only at intersections
D) Only if there are other vehicles around

12. If a traffic officer is directing you to do something against standard traffic rules, what should you do?
A) Ignore them and follow the rules
B) Follow the officer's directions
C) Only comply if there are other drivers watching
D) Stop and wait for the officer to change their command

13. What does a yellow curb indicate?
A) You can park here freely
B) No parking allowed
C) Parking is only allowed for loading and unloading
D) Parking for emergency vehicles only

The Missouri Drivers Permit Study Book 2025

14. If another driver is tailgating you, what should you do?
A) Speed up to create distance
B) Slam on your brakes to warn them
C) Change lanes or slow down gradually to let them pass
D) Ignore them and maintain your speed

15. What is the purpose of rumble strips on the road?
A) To keep drivers awake and alert
B) To mark pedestrian crossings
C) To indicate road construction zones
D) To signal an upcoming traffic light

16. When merging onto a highway, what should you do?
A) Stop at the end of the ramp and wait for a large gap
B) Match the speed of highway traffic before merging
C) Enter at any speed you prefer
D) Turn on your hazard lights

17. What is the legal Blood Alcohol Concentration (BAC) limit for drivers 21 and over in Missouri?
A) 0.00%
B) 0.02%
C) 0.08%
D) 0.10%

18. If an animal suddenly appears in front of your car, what is the best course of action?
A) Swerve sharply to avoid it
B) Brake firmly and try to stop
C) Speed up to pass it quickly
D) Close your eyes and brace for impact

19. In Missouri, which lane should you use when driving at slower speeds on a multi-lane highway?
A) The right lane
B) The left lane
C) The center lane
D) Any lane you choose

20. What does a broken white line on the road mean?
A) Passing is allowed between lanes
B) You must stay in your lane
C) Only motorcycles can pass
D) It separates traffic moving in opposite directions

21. If a traffic signal turns yellow while you are approaching an intersection, what should you do?
A) Speed up to beat the red light
B) Stop if it is safe to do so
C) Proceed as if nothing changed
D) Stop only if other cars are stopped

22. When driving through a work zone, what should you expect?
A) Reduced speed limits
B) Unexpected lane shifts
C) Possible road workers and equipment
D) All of the above

23. What is the proper way to enter a roundabout?
A) Slow down, yield to traffic, and enter when clear
B) Stop and wait for a green light
C) Speed up to merge quickly
D) Enter immediately regardless of traffic

24. If you are driving in heavy rain and visibility is limited, what should you do?
A) Turn on your high beams
B) Increase your speed to pass other cars
C) Pull over if conditions are too dangerous
D) Drive without headlights to reduce glare

25. If your car breaks down on the highway, what is the first thing you should do?
A) Exit the vehicle and wave down passing cars
B) Pull over to the right shoulder if possible
C) Call a tow truck immediately without moving
D) Abandon the vehicle and walk for help

Answer Key & Explanations
1. A) Treat it like a four-way stop.
2. B) Turn wheels **away** from the curb when parking uphill.
3. C) Missouri law requires headlights when using wipers.
4. B) Always move to the right for emergency vehicles.
5. B) Double solid yellow lines mean **no passing**.
6. B) Hydroplaning is the biggest risk on wet roads.
7. B) A flashing red light means stop before proceeding.
8. B) Steer in the direction you want to go in a skid.
9. A) You must **move over** for emergency vehicles.
10. B) Continue to the next exit.
11. B) Use turn signals at least **100 feet** before a turn.
12. B) Follow the directions of a traffic officer.

13. C) A yellow curb means **loading/unloading** only.
14. C) Slow down or change lanes to let a tailgater pass.
15. A) Rumble strips help keep drivers alert.
16. B) Match highway speed before merging.
17. C) 0.08% is the BAC limit for drivers over 21.
18. B) Brake firmly to stop safely for an animal.
19. A) The **right lane** is for slower traffic.
20. A) Broken white lines mean **lane changes are allowed**.
21. B) Stop if it is safe when a light turns yellow.
22. D) Work zones can include speed changes and lane shifts.
23. A) Yield to traffic in the roundabout before entering.
24. C) Pull over if heavy rain reduces visibility.
25. B) Pull over to the right shoulder if possible.

8.4 PRACTICE TEST 4

(25 multiple-choice questions, passing score: 80% or at least 20 correct answers)

Instructions:
- Read each question carefully and choose the **best** answer.
- There is only **one correct answer** for each question.
- Answer as if you were taking the real test.

---

1. What is the main purpose of a shared center turn lane?
A) To allow vehicles from both directions to make left turns
B) To serve as a passing lane for slower vehicles
C) To allow emergency vehicles to pass through traffic
D) To be used for U-turns only

---

2. If you are involved in a minor traffic accident with no injuries, what should you do first?
A) Leave the scene immediately
B) Move your vehicle out of traffic if possible
C) Call 911 and wait in your car
D) Wait for law enforcement without moving your car

---

3. What should you do if your brakes fail while driving?
A) Pump the brake pedal, shift to a lower gear, and use the parking brake
B) Accelerate to maintain control
C) Honk your horn and turn off the ignition
D) Continue driving until you find a repair shop

---

4. What does a solid white line between lanes indicate?
A) You can pass freely
B) Passing is discouraged but not illegal
C) You must stay in your lane unless necessary
D) It separates traffic moving in opposite directions

---

5. When should you yield the right-of-way to pedestrians at a crosswalk?
A) Only if they are already crossing
B) Only at intersections with traffic lights
C) Always, whether they are in the crosswalk or preparing to cross
D) Only if they are children or elderly

---

6. If you need to make a right turn at a red light, what must you do first?
A) Slow down and proceed without stopping
B) Stop completely and yield to traffic and pedestrians
C) Honk to alert other drivers before turning
D) Speed up to clear the intersection quickly

The Missouri Drivers Permit Study Book 2025

7. What is the legal following distance between you and the vehicle ahead in Missouri?
A) At least one car length
B) At least two seconds behind
C) At least three to four seconds behind
D) One second for every 10 mph of speed

8. When should you use your high-beam headlights?
A) In foggy conditions for better visibility
B) At night when there are no oncoming vehicles
C) In city traffic at all times
D) When driving behind another vehicle

9. What does a red arrow traffic signal mean?
A) You must stop and wait for a green arrow before turning
B) You may turn right if the intersection is clear
C) You may turn left after yielding
D) The lane is closed for turning

10. If a school bus has its red lights flashing and stop arm extended, what must you do?
A) Slow down and pass carefully
B) Stop only if children are visible
C) Stop and remain stopped until the lights turn off and the arm retracts
D) Only stop if you are traveling in the same direction as the bus

11. What should you do if an oncoming vehicle has its high beams on?
A) Flash your headlights quickly
B) Look slightly to the right of the road
C) Turn on your own high beams
D) Slow down and pull over

12. If your vehicle begins to hydroplane, what is the best action to take?
A) Slam on the brakes to slow down
B) Steer sharply to maintain control
C) Ease off the accelerator and steer straight
D) Turn the wheel back and forth quickly

13. What is the best way to check your blind spots before changing lanes?
A) Check your rearview mirror
B) Check both side mirrors
C) Look over your shoulder
D) Use your turn signals

14. When are you required to stop for a stopped school bus on a two-lane road?

A) Only if you are traveling in the same direction as the bus
B) Always, regardless of which direction you are coming from
C) Only if there are children near the road
D) Only in rural areas

15. If you are driving below the speed limit on a highway and cars are building up behind you, what should you do?
A) Maintain your speed
B) Pull over or change lanes to let traffic pass
C) Speed up to match the cars behind you
D) Stop until traffic clears

16. What does a pentagon-shaped traffic sign indicate?
A) No passing zone
B) Railroad crossing
C) School zone
D) Stop sign

17. When must you dim your high beams when approaching another vehicle?
A) At least 500 feet before an oncoming vehicle
B) At least 300 feet before an oncoming vehicle
C) Only if the other driver flashes their lights
D) Only in well-lit areas

18. What does a yield sign mean?
A) Stop completely before proceeding
B) Proceed as normal unless another car is present
C) Slow down and be prepared to stop if necessary
D) Speed up to merge quickly

19. What is the safest way to exit a highway?
A) Slow down on the highway before exiting
B) Move into the exit lane well ahead of time
C) Stop completely before entering the exit ramp
D) Cut across lanes at the last minute

20. What should you do if you are pulled over by a police officer?
A) Stop as quickly as possible in the middle of the road
B) Drive until you reach a gas station before stopping
C) Pull over to a safe location and remain in your car
D) Exit the vehicle and walk toward the officer

21. If a tire blows out while driving, what should you do?
A) Brake immediately and pull over
B) Hold the steering wheel firmly and ease off the gas

C) Turn the wheel quickly to maintain control
D) Accelerate to keep the car moving straight

22. What should you do if you are at an intersection and the traffic light turns green?
A) Proceed immediately without checking surroundings
B) Look both ways before entering the intersection
C) Honk your horn before moving forward
D) Slow down to a stop before proceeding

23. When can you legally drive on the shoulder of the road?
A) Only in emergencies or when directed by police
B) When traffic is heavy and you need to pass
C) Only if you are turning right
D) Whenever it seems safe

24. If your vehicle starts to skid, what should you do first?
A) Pump the brakes repeatedly
B) Turn the steering wheel in the direction of the skid
C) Hold the wheel straight and press the gas pedal
D) Steer in the opposite direction of the skid

25. If you are driving in a funeral procession with headlights on, what must other drivers do?
A) Merge into the procession
B) Yield and allow the procession to pass
C) Drive through the procession carefully
D) Honk to alert drivers of your presence

Answer Key & Explanations
1. What is the main purpose of a shared center turn lane?
Answer: A) To allow vehicles from both directions to make left turns
- A shared center turn lane is designed for left-turning vehicles from either direction to safely wait before completing their turn. It is not for passing, emergency vehicles, or U-turns only.

2. If you are involved in a minor traffic accident with no injuries, what should you do first?
Answer: B) Move your vehicle out of traffic if possible
- If the accident is minor and there are no injuries, move vehicles to a safe location to avoid blocking traffic and reduce the risk of further collisions.

3. What should you do if your brakes fail while driving?
Answer: A) Pump the brake pedal, shift to a lower gear, and use the parking brake

- Pumping the brakes may restore hydraulic pressure. Downshifting helps slow the vehicle, and the parking brake (applied gradually) can assist in stopping.

4. What does a solid white line between lanes indicate?
Answer: C) You must stay in your lane unless necessary
- A solid white line discourages lane changes but allows them if needed (e.g., avoiding hazards). It does not indicate opposite-direction traffic (that's a yellow line).

5. When should you yield the right-of-way to pedestrians at a crosswalk?
Answer: C) Always, whether they are in the crosswalk or preparing to cross
- Drivers must yield to pedestrians in or entering a crosswalk, regardless of traffic signals or the pedestrian's age.

6. If you need to make a right turn at a red light, what must you do first?
Answer: B) Stop completely and yield to traffic and pedestrians
- After a full stop, ensure the turn is safe and legal (unless a sign prohibits it). Yield to all oncoming traffic and crossing pedestrians.

7. What is the legal following distance between you and the vehicle ahead in Missouri?
Answer: B) At least two seconds behind
- The "two-second rule" (three to four seconds in poor conditions) ensures enough space to react if the leading vehicle stops suddenly.

8. When should you use your high-beam headlights?
Answer: B) At night when there are no oncoming vehicles
- High beams improve visibility in dark areas but must be dimmed within 500 feet of oncoming traffic or 300 feet behind another vehicle.

9. What does a red arrow traffic signal mean?
Answer: A) You must stop and wait for a green arrow before turning
- A red arrow prohibits turning in the indicated direction until the signal changes. It does not allow a yield or right turn (unless a sign permits it).

10. If a school bus has its red lights flashing and stop arm extended, what must you do?
Answer: C) Stop and remain stopped until the lights turn off and the arm retracts
- All traffic (both directions on a two-lane road) must stop for a school bus loading/unloading children, except on divided highways.

11. What should you do if an oncoming vehicle has its high beams on?
Answer: B) Look slightly to the right of the road

- Avoid staring at the bright lights. Glance toward the right edge of your lane to maintain position until the vehicle passes.

12. If your vehicle begins to hydroplane, what is the best action to take?
Answer: C) Ease off the accelerator and steer straight
- Sudden braking or steering can worsen hydroplaning. Gradually reduce speed and hold the wheel straight until traction returns.

13. What is the best way to check your blind spots before changing lanes?
Answer: C) Look over your shoulder
- Mirrors may not show all blind spots. A quick shoulder check ensures no vehicles are hidden from view.

14. When are you required to stop for a stopped school bus on a two-lane road?
Answer: B) Always, regardless of which direction you are coming from
- On undivided roads, all lanes must stop for a school bus with flashing red lights, even if traveling in the opposite direction.

15. If you are driving below the speed limit on a highway and cars are building up behind you, what should you do?
Answer: B) Pull over or change lanes to let traffic pass
- Impeding traffic can cause hazards. Move right or use a turnout to allow faster vehicles to pass safely.

16. What does a pentagon-shaped traffic sign indicate?
Answer: C) School zone
- A pentagon signals a school zone or crossing. Drivers should watch for children and obey reduced speed limits.

17. When must you dim your high beams when approaching another vehicle?
Answer: A) At least 500 feet before an oncoming vehicle
- High beams must be dimmed within 500 feet of oncoming traffic or 300 feet behind a vehicle to avoid blinding others.

18. What does a yield sign mean?
Answer: C) Slow down and be prepared to stop if necessary
- A yield sign requires drivers to give the right-of-way to other traffic or pedestrians but does not always mandate a full stop.

19. What is the safest way to exit a highway?
Answer: B) Move into the exit lane well ahead of time
- Plan lane changes early, signal, and adjust speed gradually to exit smoothly without abrupt maneuvers.

20. What should you do if you are pulled over by a police officer?
Answer: C) Pull over to a safe location and remain in your car
- Signal, stop in a safe spot, keep hands visible, and wait for instructions. Exiting the vehicle may be seen as a threat.

21. If a tire blows out while driving, what should you do?
Answer: B) Hold the steering wheel firmly and ease off the gas
- Avoid braking hard. Maintain control by gripping the wheel and coasting to a stop with gradual deceleration.

22. What should you do if you are at an intersection and the traffic light turns green?
Answer: B) Look both ways before entering the intersection
- Check for red-light runners, pedestrians, or emergency vehicles before proceeding to avoid collisions.

23. When can you legally drive on the shoulder of the road?
Answer: A) Only in emergencies or when directed by police
- Shoulders are for emergencies, breakdowns, or official instructions. They are not for passing or routine travel.

24. If your vehicle starts to skid, what should you do first?
Answer: B) Turn the steering wheel in the direction of the skid
- Steering into the skid (e.g., left if the rear slides left) helps realign the vehicle. Avoid braking or accelerating abruptly.

25. If you are driving in a funeral procession with headlights on, what must other drivers do?
Answer: B) Yield and allow the procession to pass
- Funeral processions have the right-of-way. Other drivers should not disrupt the line of vehicles, even if traffic signals change.

8.5 PRACTICE TEST 5

(25 multiple-choice questions, passing score: 80% or at least 20 correct answers)

Instructions:
- Read each question carefully and choose the **best** answer.
- There is only **one correct answer** for each question.
- Answer as if you were taking the real test.

1. What is the maximum speed limit on rural Missouri highways unless otherwise posted?
A) 55 mph
B) 60 mph
C) 65 mph
D) 70 mph

2. When parking downhill with a curb, which way should you turn your wheels?
A) Toward the curb
B) Away from the curb
C) Straight ahead
D) It does not matter

3. If an emergency vehicle with flashing lights is approaching behind you, what should you do?
A) Speed up to get out of its way
B) Pull over to the right and stop
C) Continue driving normally
D) Move to the left lane and slow down

4. At what blood alcohol concentration (BAC) level is it illegal for drivers 21 and older to operate a vehicle in Missouri?
A) 0.02%
B) 0.04%
C) 0.08%
D) 0.10%

5. What does a flashing yellow traffic light mean?
A) Stop and wait for a green light
B) Slow down and proceed with caution
C) The traffic signal is out of order
D) Only school buses must stop

6. When must you use your turn signal before making a turn in Missouri?
A) At least 50 feet before turning
B) At least 100 feet before turning

C) Only if other cars are present
D) At least five seconds before turning

7. What should you do when merging onto a highway?
A) Stop and wait for an opening
B) Accelerate to match the speed of traffic
C) Merge as slowly as possible
D) Turn on hazard lights before merging

8. If you miss your exit on the highway, what should you do?
A) Stop and back up carefully
B) Continue to the next exit
C) Make a U-turn across the median
D) Pull over and wait for traffic to clear

9. Who has the right-of-way at a four-way stop if multiple vehicles arrive at the same time?
A) The vehicle on the left
B) The largest vehicle
C) The vehicle on the right
D) The vehicle that honks first

10. What does a diamond-shaped road sign indicate?
A) Regulatory signs
B) Warning signs
C) Guide signs
D) No-passing zones

11. If you are driving at night and a vehicle is approaching with high beams on, what should you do?
A) Flash your high beams
B) Look at the center line of the road
C) Look slightly to the right
D) Close your eyes briefly to adjust

12. What is the first thing you should do if your vehicle starts skidding?
A) Slam on the brakes
B) Turn the steering wheel in the opposite direction of the skid
C) Take your foot off the gas and steer in the direction of the skid
D) Accelerate to regain control

13. When can you legally pass another vehicle on the right in Missouri?
A) When the vehicle ahead is making a left turn
B) When you are in a no-passing zone
C) On a narrow road with no center line
D) When the vehicle ahead is going below the speed limit

The Missouri Drivers Permit Study Book 2025

14. When are road conditions most slippery?
A) During a heavy rainstorm
B) Right after it starts raining
C) On a hot summer day
D) When snow has been cleared from the road

15. If you are making a left turn at an intersection and the traffic light turns green, what should you do?
A) Proceed immediately
B) Yield to oncoming traffic before turning
C) Speed up to turn before oncoming traffic reaches you
D) Only turn if a sign allows it

16. If a railroad crossing has flashing red lights, but no barrier, what must you do?
A) Slow down and proceed if you don't see a train
B) Stop only if other vehicles are stopping
C) Stop completely and wait until the lights stop flashing
D) Proceed if you've waited at least 15 seconds

17. What does a yellow pennant-shaped sign indicate?
A) A school zone ahead
B) A no-passing zone
C) A railroad crossing
D) A construction zone

18. What is the Missouri "Move Over" law?
A) Drivers must move over for faster traffic
B) Drivers must move to the left lane when passing a school bus
C) Drivers must slow down or change lanes for emergency vehicles on the roadside
D) Drivers must move over when exiting the highway

19. What is the speed limit in a school zone during school hours unless otherwise posted?
A) 10 mph
B) 15 mph
C) 20 mph
D) 25 mph

20. If an intersection has no stop signs or traffic signals, who has the right-of-way?
A) The driver who gets there first
B) The driver on the right

C) The driver on the left
D) The driver going straight

21. What should you do if your car stalls on a railroad track and a train is approaching?
A) Stay inside and call 911
B) Get out and run in the direction of the train
C) Get out and run **away** from the train at an angle
D) Try to push the car off the tracks

22. What does a solid yellow line on your side of the centerline mean?
A) Passing is allowed with caution
B) Passing is not allowed
C) Passing is only allowed at intersections
D) You can pass but must use a turn signal

23. When driving in fog, what should you do?
A) Use high beams for better visibility
B) Use low beams or fog lights
C) Drive at normal speed to keep up with traffic
D) Honk frequently to alert other drivers

24. If a police officer signals you to stop, but you are in heavy traffic with no safe place to pull over, what should you do?
A) Stop immediately, even if in traffic
B) Keep driving until the officer leaves
C) Signal and find a safe place to pull over
D) Ignore the signal if no violation occurred

25. What should you do when driving through a work zone?
A) Speed up to avoid delays
B) Slow down and follow posted work zone signs
C) Ignore construction signs if workers aren't present
D) Use your horn to warn workers

Answer Key & Explanations
1. What is the maximum speed limit on rural Missouri highways unless otherwise posted?
Answer: B) 60 mph
- Missouri's default speed limit on rural highways is **60 mph**, unless signs indicate otherwise. Some interstates may allow higher speeds (e.g., 70 mph).

2. When parking downhill with a curb, which way should you turn your wheels?
Answer: A) Toward the curb

The Missouri Drivers Permit Study Book 2025

- Turning wheels **toward the curb** ensures the car rolls into the curb if brakes fail, preventing it from entering traffic.

3. If an emergency vehicle with flashing lights is approaching behind you, what should you do?
Answer: B) Pull over to the right and stop
- Yield to emergency vehicles by pulling over to the **rightmost edge** of the road and stopping until they pass.

4. At what blood alcohol concentration (BAC) level is it illegal for drivers 21 and older to operate a vehicle in Missouri?
Answer: C) 0.08%
- The legal limit for drivers 21+ is **0.08% BAC**. For commercial drivers, it's 0.04%, and for underage drivers, it's 0.02%.

5. What does a flashing yellow traffic light mean?
Answer: B) Slow down and proceed with caution
- A flashing yellow light warns drivers to **proceed carefully** after yielding to pedestrians and other traffic.

6. When must you use your turn signal before making a turn in Missouri?
Answer: B) At least 100 feet before turning
- Missouri law requires signaling **at least 100 feet** before a turn to alert other drivers.

7. What should you do when merging onto a highway?
Answer: B) Accelerate to match the speed of traffic
- Match the highway's speed to merge smoothly. Stopping or merging too slowly creates hazards.

8. If you miss your exit on the highway, what should you do?
Answer: B) Continue to the next exit
- Never stop, back up, or U-turn. **Proceed to the next exit** and turn around safely.

9. Who has the right-of-way at a four-way stop if multiple vehicles arrive at the same time?
Answer: C) The vehicle on the right
- When vehicles arrive simultaneously, yield to the **driver on your right**.

10. What does a diamond-shaped road sign indicate?
Answer: B) Warning signs
- Diamond-shaped signs warn of hazards like curves, intersections, or pedestrian crossings.

The Missouri Drivers Permit Study Book 2025

11. If you are driving at night and a vehicle is approaching with high beams on, what should you do?
Answer: C) **Look slightly to the right**
- Avoid glare by focusing on the **right edge of your lane** until the vehicle passes.

12. What is the first thing you should do if your vehicle starts skidding?
Answer: C) **Take your foot off the gas and steer in the direction of the skid**
- Ease off the accelerator and **steer into the skid** to regain control. Avoid braking sharply.

13. When can you legally pass another vehicle on the right in Missouri?
Answer: A) **When the vehicle ahead is making a left turn**
- Passing on the right is allowed **only if the left-turning vehicle is blocking the lane** and it's safe.

14. When are road conditions most slippery?
Answer: B) **Right after it starts raining**
- Oil and dust mix with water **in the first 10–15 minutes of rain**, creating slick surfaces.

15. If you are making a left turn at an intersection and the traffic light turns green, what should you do?
Answer: B) **Yield to oncoming traffic before turning**
- A green light means **yield to oncoming traffic and pedestrians** before completing your turn.

16. If a railroad crossing has flashing red lights, but no barrier, what must you do?
Answer: C) **Stop completely and wait until the lights stop flashing**
- Flashing red lights at a crossing mean **stop and wait** until signals deactivate, even if no train is visible.

17. What does a yellow pennant-shaped sign indicate?
Answer: B) **A no-passing zone**
- Pennant-shaped signs mark the start of a **no-passing zone** (usually on the left side of the road).

18. What is the Missouri "Move Over" law?
Answer: C) **Drivers must slow down or change lanes for emergency vehicles on the roadside**
- The law requires drivers to **move over or slow down** for stopped emergency vehicles, tow trucks, or maintenance crews.

19. What is the speed limit in a school zone during school hours unless otherwise posted?

Answer: C) 20 mph
- Missouri's default school zone speed is **20 mph** when children are present (unless signs specify otherwise).

20. If an intersection has no stop signs or traffic signals, who has the right-of-way?
Answer: B) The driver on the right
- At uncontrolled intersections, yield to the **vehicle on your right**.

21. What should you do if your car stalls on a railroad track and a train is approaching?
Answer: C) Get out and run away from the train at an angle
- Exit immediately and **run diagonally away** from the tracks to avoid debris if the train hits your car.

22. What does a solid yellow line on your side of the centerline mean?
Answer: B) Passing is not allowed
- A solid yellow line prohibits passing. Cross only for turns or obstructions.

23. When driving in fog, what should you do?
Answer: B) Use low beams or fog lights
- High beams reflect off fog, reducing visibility. **Low beams or fog lights** are safer.

24. If a police officer signals you to stop, but you are in heavy traffic with no safe place to pull over, what should you do?
Answer: C) Signal and find a safe place to pull over
- **Acknowledge the officer** (e.g., hazard lights), then proceed slowly to a safe spot to stop.

25. What should you do when driving through a work zone?
Answer: B) Slow down and follow posted work zone signs
- Reduce speed, obey signs, and stay alert for workers. Fines double in work zones.

The Missouri Drivers Permit Study Book 2025

8.6 LONG PRACTICE TEST

Below is a comprehensive 160-question practice test designed to simulate the Missouri Driver's Permit Test. This batch of questions covers topics such as traffic laws, road signs, right-of-way, safe driving techniques, parking, and more. After the questions, you'll find an answer key with brief explanations for each item. Use this test to gauge your readiness and review any areas that need further study. Good luck with your preparation!

(160 multiple-choice questions. Read each question carefully and choose the best answer. There is only one correct answer per question.)

Instructions:
- Answer all 160 questions.
- Each question has four answer options labeled A, B, C, and D.
- Work through the test as if it were the real permit exam.
- When you have finished, check your responses against the answer key and review explanations for any errors.

1. What is the primary purpose of Missouri's Graduated Driver Licensing program?
A) To allow unrestricted driving for teens
B) To provide new drivers with a gradual introduction to driving responsibilities
C) To enforce strict penalties on all drivers under 18
D) To limit the number of drivers on the road

2. Which document is essential for proving your identity when applying for a permit?
A) A library card
B) A birth certificate
C) A utility bill
D) A school transcript

3. What is the minimum age required to apply for an instruction permit in Missouri?
A) 14 years old
B) 15 years old
C) 16 years old
D) 17 years old

4. Which of the following is NOT a component of the Missouri Driver's Permit Test?
A) Written Knowledge Test
B) Vision Test
C) Road Skills Test
D) Traffic Sign Identification

The Missouri Drivers Permit Study Book 2025

5. What is the minimum passing score on the Missouri written knowledge test?
A) 60%
B) 70%
C) 80%
D) 90%

6. How many multiple-choice questions are typically on the Missouri permit test?
A) 20
B) 25
C) 30
D) 35

7. What type of questions does the Missouri permit test primarily include?
A) Essay questions
B) True/False questions
C) Multiple-choice questions
D) Fill-in-the-blank questions

8. Which website is the official source for the Missouri Driver Guide?
A) Missouri Department of Revenue website
B) Missouri DMV Fan Page
C) Local library website
D) Federal Motor Carrier Safety Administration website

9. Before taking the permit test, you should study the Missouri Driver Guide because it contains:
A) Local restaurant reviews
B) Detailed explanations of traffic laws, road signs, and safe driving practices
C) Information on car models
D) Tips for buying a car

10. The Missouri permit test is administered at:
A) Public libraries
B) Missouri State Highway Patrol examination stations
C) School cafeterias
D) City hall

11. What does a red octagonal sign indicate?
A) Yield
B) Stop
C) No passing zone
D) Speed limit

12. A yellow diamond-shaped sign is used for:
A) Warning of potential hazards
B) Indicating speed limits
C) Mandatory actions
D) Providing directional guidance

13. What color are most regulatory signs in Missouri?
A) Green
B) Red
C) Blue
D) Yellow

14. A white rectangular sign generally provides:
A) Warning information
B) Informational or guide directions
C) Mandatory orders
D) Traffic light instructions

15. Which of these is a regulatory sign?
A) Stop sign
B) Curve warning sign
C) Animal crossing sign
D) Recreational area sign

16. At a four-way stop, if you arrive simultaneously with another driver, who has the right-of-way?
A) The driver on the left
B) The driver on the right
C) The driver who honks first
D) The driver with the larger vehicle

17. When approaching a yield sign, you must:
A) Slow down and prepare to stop if necessary
B) Speed up to pass the intersection
C) Ignore it if there is no cross traffic
D) Stop regardless of traffic

18. What does a flashing red traffic light require you to do?
A) Slow down and continue
B) Stop completely, then proceed when safe
C) Ignore it
D) Proceed with caution without stopping

19. A flashing yellow traffic light means:
A) Stop completely
B) Slow down and proceed with caution
C) The signal is out of order
D) Yield only to pedestrians

20. What is the purpose of a pedestrian crosswalk?
A) To indicate a no-parking zone
B) To designate an area for pedestrians to cross safely
C) To signal a turning lane
D) To indicate a school zone

21. At an intersection with a non-functioning traffic signal, you should:
A) Treat it as a four-way stop

B) Drive normally
C) Ignore it
D) Increase your speed

22. When approaching a stop sign, you must:
A) Slow down but not stop if clear
B) Come to a complete stop before proceeding
C) Yield only if another car is present
D) Honk your horn before stopping

23. Which sign indicates a change in the speed limit?
A) Diamond-shaped warning sign
B) Rectangular regulatory sign
C) Octagonal sign
D) Circular sign

24. What is the standard speed limit on most urban roads in Missouri unless posted otherwise?
A) 20 mph
B) 25-35 mph
C) 40 mph
D) 45 mph

25. What is the standard speed limit on Missouri's rural highways (unless otherwise posted)?
A) 55 mph
B) 60 mph
C) 65 mph
D) 70 mph

26. A solid yellow line along the center of the road means:
A) You may pass if clear
B) No passing allowed
C) Passing allowed only on the right
D) Stop at the line

27. A broken yellow line on your side means:
A) You may pass if it is safe
B) No passing allowed
C) Only trucks may pass
D) Pedestrians crossing

28. If you see a broken white line between lanes, it indicates:
A) You must remain in your lane
B) You may change lanes when safe
C) Passing is prohibited
D) The lane is for emergency vehicles only

29. What does a "Do Not Enter" sign mean?
A) You must stop immediately
B) You are entering a one-way street in the wrong direction

C) You are allowed to turn right
D) Speed up to exit the area

30. What should you do if you encounter a school bus with its flashing red lights and stop arm extended?
A) Slow down and pass carefully
B) Stop regardless of your direction of travel
C) Only stop if children are present
D) Honk to alert the bus driver

31. When driving, maintaining a safe following distance is essential because:
A) It improves fuel efficiency
B) It reduces the risk of rear-end collisions
C) It increases speed
D) It makes overtaking easier

32. The "three-second rule" is used to:
A) Determine how long to signal before turning
B) Ensure a safe following distance
C) Measure the time to cross a street
D) Count the seconds before accelerating

33. When approaching a roundabout, you should:
A) Speed up to merge quickly
B) Yield to vehicles already in the roundabout
C) Stop completely before entering
D) Ignore the roundabout if no signs are posted

34. In a roundabout, which direction do vehicles travel in Missouri?
A) Clockwise
B) Counterclockwise
C) Either direction
D) It depends on the sign

35. What is the primary purpose of rumble strips on highways?
A) To mark the edge of the road
B) To alert drowsy drivers and keep them awake
C) To separate lanes
D) To indicate an upcoming exit

36. When passing another vehicle, you should:
A) Accelerate suddenly
B) Maintain a safe distance and signal before changing lanes
C) Cut in quickly
D) Flash your lights continuously

37. What should you do if you are tailgated?
A) Slam on your brakes
B) Speed up excessively
C) Increase your following distance or change lanes to let them pass
D) Honk continuously

38. When making a left turn at an intersection, you must yield to:
A) Oncoming traffic and pedestrians
B) Vehicles in your lane only
C) Cyclists only
D) Traffic behind you

39. The proper hand signal for a left turn is:
A) Left arm extended straight out
B) Left arm bent upward at a 90-degree angle
C) Left arm bent downward at a 90-degree angle
D) Right arm extended straight out

40. When backing up, you should:
A) Rely solely on your backup camera
B) Look over your shoulder and use mirrors
C) Drive as quickly as possible
D) Keep both hands off the wheel

41. What is hydroplaning?
A) When your car's brakes fail
B) When your tires lose contact with the road surface due to water
C) When your engine overheats
D) When your car swerves due to wind

42. If you begin to hydroplane, you should:
A) Slam on the brakes
B) Accelerate to regain traction
C) Ease off the gas and steer straight
D) Turn the steering wheel abruptly

43. What is the proper technique for emergency braking in a vehicle with ABS?
A) Pump the brakes repeatedly
B) Press the brake pedal firmly and hold it
C) Use only the parking brake
D) Brake and then accelerate quickly

44. When driving in fog, you should use:
A) High beam headlights
B) Low beam headlights
C) Hazard lights continuously
D) No headlights

45. In Missouri, when are you required to use your headlights?
A) Only at night
B) From 30 minutes after sunset until 30 minutes before sunrise and during poor visibility
C) Only in rural areas
D) Only when approaching intersections

46. What does the "Move Over" law require you to do?
A) Change lanes to the left when passing any vehicle

B) Slow down and, if safe, move over for a stopped emergency vehicle or tow truck
C) Stop immediately upon seeing a stopped vehicle
D) Increase speed when passing a work zone

47. What should you do if your vehicle stalls on the highway?
A) Attempt to restart immediately while in traffic
B) Pull over to the shoulder safely and turn on your hazard lights
C) Exit the vehicle in heavy traffic
D) Continue driving slowly

48. What is the significance of a "No U-Turn" sign?
A) It means you can make a U-turn if there's no oncoming traffic
B) It prohibits U-turns at that location
C) It indicates a U-turn lane is available
D) It only applies to trucks

49. A "Yield" sign instructs you to:
A) Stop completely
B) Slow down and give right-of-way to vehicles and pedestrians
C) Proceed without caution
D) Increase speed

50. What is the purpose of a speed limit sign?
A) To provide directions to the nearest city
B) To indicate the maximum speed legally allowed under normal conditions
C) To suggest a safe speed for all weather conditions
D) To warn of upcoming curves

51. If you are driving and become fatigued, what is the best course of action?
A) Continue driving and listen to music loudly
B) Increase speed to reach your destination faster
C) Pull over safely and take a break or a short nap
D) Drink a caffeinated beverage and keep driving

52. Which of the following is a distraction that should be avoided while driving?
A) Adjusting mirrors before departure
B) Texting or using a cell phone without a hands-free system
C) Listening to a low-volume radio
D) Using GPS before starting your journey

53. When approaching a railroad crossing, you should:
A) Speed up to cross quickly
B) Slow down and look both ways for an approaching train
C) Stop only if you see a train
D) Honk to clear the tracks

54. What does a red curb typically indicate?
A) A loading zone for commercial vehicles
B) Parking is prohibited

C) Reserved parking for disabled drivers only
D) Free parking

55. What should you do if you see a pedestrian crossing outside of a marked crosswalk?
A) Speed up to pass before they cross
B) Slow down and yield, as pedestrians have the right-of-way
C) Ignore them since they are not in a designated area
D) Honk to alert them

56. When you are driving in a work zone, you should:
A) Maintain the same speed as before
B) Increase your speed to get through quickly
C) Reduce your speed and follow posted work zone signs
D) Drive in the left lane only

57. What does a "No Parking" sign mean?
A) Parking is allowed for a limited time
B) Parking is prohibited in that area
C) You can stop briefly to load or unload
D) Parking is only allowed for commercial vehicles

58. If you are in a construction zone, you may be subject to:
A) Reduced speed limits and higher fines for speeding
B) Free parking only
C) No restrictions
D) Only a verbal warning for speeding

59. What is the purpose of a "Do Not Pass" zone?
A) To indicate where passing is allowed
B) To warn that passing is prohibited due to safety hazards
C) To mark a rest area
D) To signal a school zone

60. When approaching a pedestrian crossing, you should:
A) Speed up if no pedestrians are visible
B) Slow down and prepare to stop if pedestrians are present
C) Honk to warn pedestrians
D) Ignore it if the crossing is unmarked

61. In Missouri, when driving on an interstate, you should always:
A) Stay in the left lane regardless of speed
B) Keep right unless passing
C) Drive in the center lane
D) Switch lanes frequently

62. If a police officer directs you to pull over, you should:
A) Immediately pull over to a safe area and remain in your vehicle
B) Speed up to avoid being stopped
C) Continue driving until you see a gas station
D) Stop in the middle of the road

63. When using a cell phone while driving in Missouri, which method is acceptable?
A) Handheld texting
B) Using a hands-free system
C) Browsing social media
D) Making video calls

64. What does a "No U-Turn" sign look like?
A) A circular sign with a red line crossing an arrow
B) A triangular sign with a U shape
C) A rectangular sign with the words "No U-Turn"
D) A diamond-shaped sign with a U-turn arrow

65. When turning right on red in Missouri, you must:
A) Stop completely, then turn if the way is clear
B) Proceed without stopping
C) Only signal and then turn
D) Yield to oncoming traffic only

66. What does a "One Way" sign indicate?
A) You can drive in both directions
B) Traffic must travel only in the direction indicated
C) It is a pedestrian-only street
D) U-turns are allowed

67. When merging onto a highway from an on-ramp, you should:
A) Stop at the end of the ramp
B) Accelerate to match the speed of traffic
C) Turn on your hazard lights and wait
D) Enter at a lower speed than highway traffic

68. Which of the following factors affects your stopping distance?
A) Your vehicle's weight
B) Road conditions
C) Your reaction time
D) All of the above

69. What is a safe method to change lanes on a highway?
A) Signal, check mirrors and blind spots, then change lanes gradually
B) Signal and change lanes abruptly
C) Do not signal if the lane appears clear
D) Use high beams as a signal

70. If you are following a large truck on a highway, you should:
A) Stay close behind it to reduce wind resistance
B) Maintain extra distance due to its large blind spots
C) Overtake quickly on the right
D) Flash your headlights to signal your presence

71. Which of the following is an example of a defensive driving technique?
A) Anticipating potential hazards by scanning the road

B) Speeding to avoid traffic
C) Tailgating to discourage slow drivers
D) Ignoring the behavior of other drivers

72. What should you do if your vehicle's tire pressure is low?
A) Continue driving until you reach your destination
B) Inflate the tires as soon as possible
C) Drive faster to generate heat in the tires
D) Only replace the tires at a service station

73. What does the term "blind spot" refer to?
A) The area behind your vehicle only
B) Areas around your vehicle that are not visible in your mirrors
C) A spot on the windshield that is smudged
D) The rearview mirror

74. Which action is recommended when exiting a parking space?
A) Accelerate immediately
B) Check mirrors and blind spots before pulling out
C) Rev the engine to signal your exit
D) Exit without checking if pedestrians are present

75. What is the safest way to pass a slower vehicle on a two-lane road?
A) Pass quickly without checking for oncoming traffic
B) Ensure a clear passing zone and signal before overtaking
C) Pass on the right regardless of the situation
D) Tailgate until the driver speeds up

76. When driving in rain, why should you avoid using cruise control?
A) It increases fuel consumption
B) It may prevent you from responding to reduced traction
C) It is illegal in Missouri
D) It causes distractions

77. If you experience a tire blowout while driving, you should:
A) Brake hard immediately
B) Maintain control by keeping a firm grip on the steering wheel and gradually slow down
C) Accelerate to stabilize the vehicle
D) Swerve sharply to avoid obstacles

78. What should you do if your headlights suddenly go out while driving at night?
A) Continue driving at the same speed
B) Pull over to a safe location and use emergency flashers
C) Switch to high beams
D) Rely on streetlights only

79. How can you prevent driver fatigue during long highway trips?
A) Listen to loud music continuously
B) Take regular breaks and get adequate rest before driving

C) Drive without a break to reach the destination faster
D) Increase the temperature inside the vehicle

80. What does the "Implied Consent Law" in Missouri mean?
A) You may refuse a breath test
B) By driving, you agree to submit to chemical tests if suspected of DUI
C) You can refuse to stop for police
D) It applies only to drivers under 21

81. Which sign indicates a pedestrian crossing ahead?
A) A rectangular blue sign
B) A yellow diamond sign with a figure walking
C) A red octagonal sign
D) A green arrow sign

82. What is the proper procedure for parallel parking?
A) Pull up beside the car ahead, reverse while turning sharply, then adjust forward
B) Speed into the space without slowing down
C) Park at an angle and then adjust
D) Reverse without checking mirrors

83. When driving on a mountain road, what is an important consideration?
A) Maintaining a high speed
B) Using engine braking on declines
C) Ignoring steep curves
D) Driving without headlights

84. In adverse weather, increasing your following distance is important because:
A) It reduces tire wear
B) It gives you more time to react to sudden stops
C) It allows you to overtake easily
D) It increases fuel economy

85. What should you do if you see an obstruction on the road ahead?
A) Swerve suddenly
B) Maintain your speed and hope for the best
C) Slow down and change lanes if safe
D) Accelerate to pass quickly

86. When approaching a construction zone, you should:
A) Drive at the posted reduced speed
B) Maintain your normal speed
C) Speed up to exit the zone quickly
D) Ignore temporary signs

87. What is the best way to handle a driver who is behaving aggressively on the road?
A) Engage with them by honking and gesturing
B) Keep a safe distance and avoid confrontation

C) Speed up to get away
D) Brake hard in front of them

88. If a traffic officer directs you to turn around on a highway, you should:
A) Stop in the middle of the road
B) Find a safe area to make the maneuver
C) Ignore the direction
D) Continue driving until you reach the next exit

89. What does the term "vehicle blind spot" refer to?
A) The area directly in front of your car
B) Areas around your vehicle that cannot be seen in your mirrors
C) The back window
D) The dashboard

90. When is it legal to pass a school bus on a two-lane road?
A) When it is moving
B) Only when its stop arm is retracted and lights are off
C) Always, if no children are present
D) Never

91. If you are driving and a tire suddenly bursts, your first action should be to:
A) Slam on the brakes
B) Hold the steering wheel firmly and decelerate gradually
C) Turn sharply to avoid a collision
D) Accelerate to stabilize the vehicle

92. Which of the following is considered a distracted driving activity?
A) Adjusting the radio before starting your trip
B) Talking on a hands-free device
C) Texting while driving
D) Using a GPS mounted on the dashboard

93. How should you respond to a flashing amber light at an intersection?
A) Treat it like a stop sign
B) Proceed with caution
C) Speed up
D) Ignore it completely

94. When driving in heavy snowfall, what is the best method to maintain control?
A) Brake hard at the first sign of snow
B) Accelerate to prevent slippage
C) Drive slowly and use gentle braking
D) Turn off the defroster

95. What does a "No Passing" sign indicate?
A) You may pass if safe
B) Passing is prohibited in that area
C) Only trucks are allowed to pass
D) Pedestrians may cross

96. How do you determine if a lane is safe for passing on a two-lane road?
A) Look for dashed centerlines
B) Check for solid double yellow lines
C) Rely solely on your speedometer
D) Guess based on traffic density

97. Which vehicle is most affected by wind while driving?
A) A sports car
B) A large truck
C) A compact car
D) A minivan

98. In a roundabout, you must yield to:
A) Vehicles already circulating
B) Pedestrians only
C) Vehicles entering from the right
D) Bicycles only

99. What does a "No Turn on Red" sign mean?
A) You must always turn right on red
B) You are not allowed to turn right when the light is red
C) You must turn left instead
D) It is a suggestion, not a rule

100. How should you prepare for a long drive to avoid fatigue?
A) Drive without taking breaks
B) Ensure you are well-rested and take periodic breaks
C) Drink several cups of coffee continuously
D) Rely on fast food for energy

101. What is the recommended practice for checking your blind spot?
A) Rely only on your side mirrors
B) Turn your head to look over your shoulder
C) Use only the rearview mirror
D) Count on other drivers to signal

102. Which action is considered aggressive driving?
A) Allowing another vehicle to merge
B) Constantly switching lanes without signaling
C) Keeping a safe following distance
D) Using turn signals properly

103. What should you do if your vehicle's engine begins to overheat?
A) Increase your speed to cool the engine
B) Turn off the air conditioning and pull over safely
C) Continue driving until the engine cools naturally
D) Open the radiator cap immediately

104. What does the "Slow Moving Vehicle" emblem on a vehicle indicate?
A) The vehicle is going at a normal speed
B) The vehicle, such as a farm tractor, is moving at a reduced speed

C) The vehicle is for emergency use only
D) The vehicle must be passed immediately

105. When driving on icy roads, what is the safest approach to braking?
A) Brake abruptly to stop quickly
B) Use gentle, progressive braking to avoid skidding
C) Avoid braking entirely
D) Brake only if another car is close

106. When driving at night, why is it important to adjust your rearview mirror to "night mode"?
A) It reduces glare from vehicles behind you
B) It makes your mirror darker
C) It increases the brightness of the lights behind you
D) It is required by law

107. What does a "No Stopping" sign indicate?
A) You may stop temporarily
B) Stopping is not permitted at any time
C) Parking is allowed but not stopping
D) Only emergency stops are allowed

108. What should you do if you encounter a pothole on the road?
A) Swerve sharply to avoid it
B) Brake abruptly
C) Maintain your course and slow down gradually
D) Speed up to minimize damage

109. Which of the following is an advantage of using a defensive driving course?
A) It allows you to skip the permit test
B) It teaches strategies to avoid accidents and improve road safety
C) It guarantees a perfect score on the test
D) It eliminates the need for a vision test

110. When approaching a school zone during active hours, you should:
A) Drive at the posted speed limit
B) Increase your speed slightly
C) Reduce your speed and be extra cautious
D) Ignore the signs if no children are visible

111. Which gear is most appropriate for ascending a steep hill in a manual vehicle?
A) High gear
B) Neutral
C) Lower gear
D) Overdrive

112. What does a "No Outlet" sign indicate?
A) The road continues but does not lead to a through route
B) You may turn around

C) There is an emergency exit
D) The road is a one-way street

113. When driving in a one-way street, you should:
A) Drive in any lane
B) Follow the direction indicated on the sign
C) Only use the left lane
D) Make U-turns if needed

114. What is the purpose of using the "Dutch Reach" technique when opening a car door?
A) To impress other drivers
B) To ensure you check for oncoming cyclists or vehicles
C) To open the door faster
D) To signal your intent to leave the vehicle

115. What does a green light indicate at a traffic signal?
A) Stop immediately
B) Proceed if the intersection is clear
C) Yield to oncoming traffic
D) Prepare to stop

116. When turning left on a green light without a protected left-turn arrow, you must yield to:
A) Pedestrians only
B) Oncoming traffic and pedestrians
C) Vehicles in the left lane only
D) None of the above

117. If you are driving and a tire suddenly blows out, what is your first priority?
A) Accelerate to stabilize the car
B) Brake hard immediately
C) Keep a firm grip on the wheel and gradually slow down
D) Swerve to avoid the blown tire

118. What is the effect of tailgating another vehicle?
A) It increases fuel efficiency
B) It reduces your stopping distance, making rear-end collisions more likely
C) It improves road visibility
D) It encourages smooth traffic flow

119. In Missouri, what is required if you are driving with a learner's permit?
A) No supervision is needed
B) You must be accompanied by a licensed driver who meets the state's requirements
C) You may drive alone during daylight hours only
D) You are allowed to drive without a supervision requirement

120. What should you do if you're driving and encounter a flooded roadway?
A) Drive through quickly to get to the other side
B) Test the depth with your foot and proceed

C) Avoid the area entirely and find an alternate route
D) Drive slowly to avoid splashing

121. What does a "Red Light Camera" sign indicate?
A) There is a camera monitoring traffic violations at the intersection
B) The intersection has a malfunctioning traffic light
C) The intersection is only for commercial vehicles
D) You should speed up before the light turns red

122. When approaching a railroad crossing with a barrier, you should:
A) Speed up to beat the train
B) Stop if the barrier is down or flashing
C) Honk to alert the train
D) Proceed if no train is visible

123. If you are involved in an accident, which of the following is required by Missouri law?
A) Leave the scene immediately
B) Exchange information with the other party
C) Only report the accident if there are injuries
D) Wait for a police officer to arrive before moving

124. When driving in heavy traffic, what is the best strategy for lane changes?
A) Change lanes frequently to keep up with the flow
B) Make gradual lane changes with proper signals and checks
C) Remain in the same lane regardless of traffic
D) Speed up to force a lane change

125. What is the correct procedure when you approach a roundabout?
A) Enter immediately without stopping
B) Stop completely before entering
C) Slow down, yield to traffic already in the circle, and enter when safe
D) Signal to merge on the right

126. What is a common cause of multi-vehicle accidents on highways?
A) Under-inflated tires
B) Tailgating and abrupt braking
C) Using cruise control
D) Driving in the left lane exclusively

127. When backing out of a parking space, you should:
A) Rely solely on your rearview camera
B) Check all mirrors and look over your shoulder
C) Drive backwards quickly
D) Signal and then reverse without checking

128. If your car starts to overheat, you should:
A) Increase your speed to cool the engine
B) Turn off the A/C, pull over safely, and allow the engine to cool
C) Continue driving to the nearest gas station
D) Open the radiator cap immediately while driving

129. What does a "No Right Turn on Red" sign indicate?
A) You may turn right on red if safe
B) Right turns on red are prohibited at that intersection
C) You must turn left instead
D) You should wait for a green arrow

130. When driving through a foggy area, why should you use low beams instead of high beams?
A) Low beams provide a wider field of vision
B) High beams reflect off the fog and reduce visibility
C) Low beams are legally required in fog
D) High beams cause glare for oncoming traffic only

131. What does a "Bicycle Lane" marking indicate?
A) Only bicycles are allowed in that lane
B) You should be extra cautious of cyclists
C) Cars may use the lane at any time
D) The lane is reserved for buses

132. When is it safe to overtake a vehicle on a two-lane road?
A) When you see a dashed center line and it is safe
B) At any time, if you feel confident
C) When the road curves sharply
D) Only in heavy traffic

133. What is the purpose of a "Check Engine" light on your dashboard?
A) It indicates that you need to get your engine tuned
B) It warns of a potential problem with your engine or emissions system
C) It shows that your fuel is low
D) It alerts you to tire pressure issues

134. If a traffic signal at an intersection is flashing red, you should:
A) Slow down and proceed with caution
B) Treat it as a stop sign and proceed when safe
C) Speed up to clear the intersection
D) Ignore the signal if no one else stops

135. What does a "No Passing Zone" look like on the road?
A) A broken yellow line
B) A solid yellow line
C) A dashed white line
D) A double solid white line

136. Which factor does NOT affect braking distance?
A) Road surface condition
B) Vehicle weight
C) Tire tread condition
D) Exterior color of the car

137. When driving on an incline, what is recommended to maintain control?
A) Use a lower gear to help with acceleration and braking

B) Use the highest gear available
C) Accelerate rapidly
D) Shift to neutral when climbing

138. What does a "No Turn on Red" sign require you to do?
A) Turn on red if no pedestrians are present
B) Not turn on red under any circumstances
C) Only turn on red during off-peak hours
D) Wait for the light to turn green

139. When encountering a merging lane on the highway, you should:
A) Maintain your speed and be prepared to adjust
B) Speed up and merge quickly
C) Stop at the merge point
D) Change lanes abruptly

140. What is the purpose of the "Seat Belt" reminder light?
A) To indicate that your car is in motion
B) To remind you and your passengers to wear seat belts
C) To show that your airbag is activated
D) To signal that you must replace your seat belts

141. Which action is essential when driving through a roundabout?
A) Accelerate quickly to clear the circle
B) Yield to traffic already in the roundabout
C) Signal only if there are pedestrians present
D) Enter without checking mirrors

142. What is the recommended action if you see a "Falling Rocks" sign on a mountainous road?
A) Maintain your current speed
B) Increase your speed to pass quickly
C) Slow down and be prepared for debris
D) Stop immediately until the sign is removed

143. When driving in rain, why is it important to avoid sudden movements?
A) Sudden movements can cause water splashing
B) They can lead to loss of traction and control
C) They can damage your car's paint
D) They are discouraged by law

144. Which of the following is NOT typically affected by adverse weather conditions?
A) Tire traction
B) Engine performance
C) Visibility
D) Vehicle color

145. What does a "Yield to Oncoming Traffic" sign at an intersection indicate?
A) You have the right-of-way
B) You must slow down and let oncoming vehicles pass

C) Stop completely regardless of traffic
D) Only yield to pedestrians

146. Which of the following best describes "defensive driving"?
A) Driving as fast as possible to avoid obstacles
B) Proactively anticipating hazards and reacting safely
C) Ignoring other drivers to focus solely on your own vehicle
D) Driving only in clear weather conditions

147. What does a "No Outlet" sign mean?
A) You can turn around freely
B) The road ends, and you should not continue
C) U-turns are allowed
D) The road is one-way

148. In adverse weather, what should you do to increase your reaction time?
A) Reduce your speed
B) Increase your following distance
C) Both A and B
D) None of the above

149. When driving in a construction zone, you should:
A) Follow the posted speed limit and be alert for workers
B) Drive at normal speeds
C) Overtake slow-moving construction vehicles
D) Ignore temporary signs if there are no workers visible

150. What is the recommended procedure if you are driving and encounter a deer crossing the road?
A) Swerve sharply to avoid it
B) Brake firmly and try to stop
C) Stay calm, slow down, and brake gradually if needed
D) Speed up to scare the deer away

151. Which of the following factors can affect a vehicle's acceleration?
A) Engine power
B) Vehicle weight
C) Road incline
D) All of the above

152. What does the term "blind spot" refer to in driving?
A) The area directly behind your car
B) Areas that cannot be seen through your mirrors
C) The area covered by your rearview mirror only
D) A portion of the road with no lighting

153. How should you react if you see an emergency vehicle stopped on the side of the road with flashing lights?
A) Speed up to pass it quickly
B) Move over or slow down as required by law

C) Continue driving at the same speed
D) Stop immediately in your lane

154. When is it legal to use a handheld cell phone while driving in Missouri?
A) When driving on the highway
B) When driving in a school zone
C) It is illegal for drivers under 21 and discouraged for others
D) Only during emergencies

155. If you are unsure of the meaning of a road sign while driving, you should:
A) Guess based on similar signs
B) Rely on your knowledge from the Missouri Driver Guide
C) Ignore the sign
D) Ask a passenger for their opinion

156. What should you do if you approach a stop sign and a vehicle is already in the intersection?
A) Proceed slowly without stopping
B) Stop completely and yield until the vehicle clears the intersection
C) Honk to alert the other driver
D) Speed up to beat the vehicle

157. When approaching a pedestrian crossing with children present, you should:
A) Sound your horn repeatedly
B) Slow down and be prepared to stop
C) Continue at the same speed
D) Accelerate to pass quickly

158. What is the correct action when you see a "No Parking" sign?
A) Stop briefly and then move
B) Do not park in the area indicated
C) Park only during off-peak hours
D) Park with the hazard lights on

159. What does a "Caution: Winding Road" sign warn you about?
A) A change in speed limit
B) Upcoming curves and potential hazards
C) Construction ahead
D) A one-way street

160. If you experience glare from the sun while driving, you should:
A) Look directly at the sun
B) Use sunglasses and adjust your visor
C) Open your windows to let in fresh air
D) Accelerate to get past the glare

The Missouri Drivers Permit Study Book 2025

Answer Key & Explanations

1. **B** – The GDL program is designed to gradually introduce new drivers to the responsibilities of driving.
2. **B** – A birth certificate is a primary document for verifying identity.
3. **B** – In Missouri, you must be at least 15 years old to apply for an instruction permit.
4. **C** – The road skills test is part of the full licensing process, not the initial permit test.
5. **C** – You must score at least 80% on the written test.
6. **B** – The Missouri permit test typically includes 25 multiple-choice questions.
7. **C** – The permit test uses multiple-choice questions to assess your knowledge.
8. **A** – The Missouri Department of Revenue website is the official source.
9. **B** – The guide details traffic laws, road signs, and safe driving practices.
10. **B** – Testing is conducted at MSHP examination stations.
11. **B** – A red octagon universally means "Stop."
12. **A** – Yellow diamond signs warn of potential hazards.
13. **B** – Most regulatory signs (like stop signs) are red.
14. **B** – White rectangular signs provide informational guidance.
15. **A** – Stop signs are regulatory signs.
16. **B** – At a four-way stop, the driver on the right has the right-of-way when arriving simultaneously.
17. **A** – You must slow down and be prepared to stop at a yield sign.
18. **B** – A flashing red light means stop completely before proceeding.
19. **B** – A flashing yellow light signals caution.
20. **B** – Crosswalks designate safe crossing areas for pedestrians.
21. **A** – Treat a non-functioning traffic signal as a four-way stop.
22. **B** – You must come to a complete stop at a stop sign.
23. **B** – Speed limit signs are rectangular and indicate maximum legal speeds.
24. **B** – Urban roads typically have limits between 25-35 mph.
25. **C** – The standard rural highway speed limit in Missouri is generally 65 mph unless posted otherwise.
26. **B** – A solid yellow line means no passing.

The Missouri Drivers Permit Study Book 2025

27. **A** – A broken yellow line on your side means you may pass if safe.
28. **B** – A broken white line indicates lane changes are permitted when safe.
29. **B** – "Do Not Enter" signs warn you not to enter a one-way street in the wrong direction.
30. **B** – You must stop for a school bus with flashing red lights and an extended stop arm.
31. **B** – Maintaining proper distance reduces the risk of rear-end collisions.
32. **B** – The three-second rule helps ensure a safe following distance.
33. **B** – You must yield to vehicles already circulating in a roundabout.
34. **B** – In Missouri roundabouts, traffic flows counterclockwise.
35. **B** – Rumble strips alert drivers and help maintain lane discipline.
36. **B** – Always signal and check mirrors before changing lanes.
37. **C** – Increase your following distance or change lanes if safe.
38. **A** – When turning left, yield to both oncoming traffic and pedestrians.
39. **A** – Extending your left arm straight out signals a left turn.
40. **B** – Look over your shoulder and check mirrors when backing up.
41. **B** – Hydroplaning occurs when water causes your tires to lose traction.
42. **C** – Ease off the gas and steer straight to regain traction when hydroplaning.
43. **B** – With ABS, press and hold the brake pedal firmly.
44. **B** – Low beam headlights are recommended in foggy conditions.
45. **B** – Headlights are required from 30 minutes after sunset until 30 minutes before sunrise and when visibility is poor.
46. **B** – The "Move Over" law mandates slowing down or changing lanes for stopped emergency vehicles.
47. **B** – Pull over safely and activate your hazard lights if your vehicle stalls.
48. **B** – "No Outlet" signs indicate that the road does not continue as a through route.
49. **B** – Yield signs instruct you to slow down and give right-of-way.
50. **B** – Speed limit signs indicate the maximum legal speed under normal conditions.
51. **C** – If fatigued, pull over safely and take a break or nap.
52. **B** – Using a handheld cell phone is a distraction and should be avoided.
53. **B** – At a railroad crossing, slow down and check both ways for trains.
54. **B** – A red curb usually means parking is prohibited.

55. **B** – Always yield to pedestrians, even if they are not in a marked crosswalk.
56. **C** – In work zones, reduce speed and follow posted signs.
57. **B** – "No Parking" means parking is prohibited in that area.
58. **A** – In construction zones, reduced speed limits and higher fines for speeding are common.
59. **B** – "No Passing" zones are established for safety on curves or hills.
60. **B** – Slow down and be prepared to stop at pedestrian crossings.
61. **B** – On interstates, you should keep right unless passing.
62. **A** – When pulled over, safely pull over and remain in your vehicle.
63. **B** – Using a hands-free system is the acceptable method for phone use.
64. **A** – A "No U-Turn" sign typically shows a U-turn crossed out by a red line.
65. **A** – When turning right on red, you must first come to a complete stop and yield.
66. **B** – "One Way" signs indicate traffic must travel in the indicated direction.
67. **B** – Match your speed with highway traffic when merging.
68. **D** – Reaction time, vehicle weight, and road conditions all affect braking distance.
69. **A** – Safe lane changes require signaling, checking mirrors, and a gradual maneuver.
70. **B** – Give extra space when following a large truck due to its blind spots.
71. **A** – Defensive driving means anticipating hazards and acting safely.
72. **B** – Low tire pressure should be corrected as soon as possible.
73. **B** – Blind spots are areas around your vehicle that your mirrors don't cover.
74. **B** – Check mirrors and blind spots before exiting a parking space.
75. **B** – Safely overtake on a two-lane road only when there's a clear passing zone.
76. **B** – Cruise control is not advised in rain because reduced traction requires active control.
77. **B** – If a tire blows out, hold the steering wheel firmly and slow down gradually.
78. **B** – If headlights fail at night, pull over safely and use your emergency flashers.

79. **B** – To avoid fatigue, take regular breaks and ensure you are well-rested.
80. **B** – The "Implied Consent Law" means that by driving, you agree to chemical testing if suspected of DUI.
81. **B** – A diamond-shaped sign with a pedestrian symbol indicates a pedestrian crossing ahead.
82. **A** – Parallel parking involves pulling up next to a vehicle, reversing with a turn, and then adjusting.
83. **B** – On mountain roads, use engine braking on declines to help control speed.
84. **B** – In adverse weather, increasing your following distance allows more reaction time.
85. **C** – Slow down and change lanes if safe when approaching an obstruction.
86. **C** – In construction zones, obey the posted speed limits and instructions.
87. **B** – Keeping a safe distance and avoiding confrontation is the safest way to handle aggressive drivers.
88. **B** – Follow the officer's directions and find a safe area to turn around if instructed.
89. **B** – A vehicle's blind spot comprises areas that cannot be seen in your mirrors.
90. **B** – On two-lane roads, you must stop for a school bus in both directions.
91. **C** – In a tire blowout, maintain control by holding the steering wheel and decelerate gradually.
92. **C** – Texting while driving is a dangerous distraction and should be avoided.
93. **B** – A flashing amber light means proceed with caution.
94. **C** – In heavy snowfall, drive slowly and brake gently to maintain control.
95. **B** – "No Passing" signs indicate that overtaking is not permitted.
96. **A** – A dashed centerline indicates that passing may be allowed when safe.
97. **B** – Large trucks are most affected by wind due to their size.
98. **A** – In a roundabout, yield to vehicles already circulating.
99. **B** – A red arrow indicates that you must not turn in that direction until it changes.
100. **B** – For long highway trips, take breaks and ensure you are well-rested.

The Missouri Drivers Permit Study Book 2025

101. **B** – Look over your shoulder to check your blind spots.
102. **B** – Aggressive driving includes constant lane switching without signaling.
103. **B** – If your engine overheats, turn off the A/C and pull over safely to let it cool.
104. **B** – The "Check Engine" light warns of potential engine or emissions issues.
105. **B** – On icy roads, use gentle, progressive braking to avoid skidding.
106. **A** – "Night mode" on rearview mirrors reduces glare from vehicles behind.
107. **B** – "No Stopping" signs mean you are not allowed to stop at any time in that area.
108. **C** – Slow down gradually when approaching a pothole to minimize impact.
109. **B** – Defensive driving courses teach techniques to prevent accidents and improve safety.
110. **C** – In a school zone, reduce your speed and be extra cautious, regardless of visible children.
111. **C** – A lower gear provides more power and control when ascending steep hills.
112. **B** – A "No Outlet" sign indicates the road does not provide a through route.
113. **B** – When driving in a one-way street, follow the direction indicated by the sign.
114. **B** – The "Dutch Reach" forces you to look over your shoulder for cyclists or oncoming traffic when opening your door.
115. **B** – A green light means you may proceed if the intersection is clear.
116. **B** – Yield to oncoming traffic and pedestrians before making a left turn on a green light without a protected arrow.
117. **C** – In the event of a tire blowout, keep a firm grip and decelerate gradually.
118. **B** – Tailgating decreases your available stopping distance, raising collision risk.
119. **B** – Permit holders must be accompanied by a licensed driver who meets Missouri requirements.
120. **C** – In a flooded roadway, avoid the area and seek an alternate route.
121. **A** – A red light camera sign warns that violations at the intersection are being monitored.

The Missouri Drivers Permit Study Book 2025

122. **B** – At a railroad crossing with a barrier, stop if the barrier is down or flashing.
123. **B** – Missouri law requires exchanging information after an accident.
124. **B** – Gradual lane changes with proper signals are safest in heavy traffic.
125. **A** – In a roundabout, yield to circulating traffic before entering.
126. **B** – Tailgating and abrupt braking are common causes of multi-vehicle highway accidents.
127. **B** – When backing out, check mirrors and look over your shoulder.
128. **B** – If overheating, turn off A/C and pull over safely; do not open the radiator cap immediately.
129. **B** – "No Right Turn on Red" means turning right on red is not permitted.
130. **B** – When merging, maintain the speed of traffic on the highway.
131. **D** – Low beams are used in fog because high beams reflect off the moisture and worsen visibility.
132. **A** – You can pass on the right if the vehicle ahead is turning left and the roadway permits it.
133. **D** – The engine's performance, along with vehicle weight and road incline, affects acceleration.
134. **B** – A flashing red light requires a complete stop before proceeding when safe.
135. **B** – A "No Passing Zone" is indicated by solid yellow lines.
136. **D** – The exterior color of the car does not affect braking distance.
137. **A** – Using a lower gear on an incline helps maintain power and control.
138. **B** – A "No Turn on Red" sign prohibits right turns on red.
139. **A** – When merging, signal, check mirrors, and adjust speed gradually.
140. **B** – The seat belt reminder light exists to prompt everyone to fasten their seat belts.
141. **B** – In a roundabout, yield to traffic already circulating.
142. **C** – When you see a "Falling Rocks" sign, slow down and be alert for debris.
143. **B** – Sudden movements in rain can cause loss of traction and control.
144. **D** – Vehicle color is not affected by weather conditions.
145. **B** – A "Yield to Oncoming Traffic" sign requires you to slow down and let vehicles pass.
146. **B** – Defensive driving involves anticipating hazards and taking preventive measures.

147. **B** – A "No Outlet" sign means the road ends or does not lead to another through route.
148. **C** – In adverse weather, reducing speed and increasing following distance gives you more reaction time.
149. **A** – In work zones, obey posted speed limits and exercise caution.
150. **C** – When encountering a deer, slow down and brake gradually without swerving abruptly.
151. **D** – Engine power, vehicle weight, and road incline all affect acceleration.
152. **B** – Blind spots are areas around your vehicle not visible in your mirrors.
153. **B** – When an emergency vehicle is stopped with flashing lights, slow down or move over as required by law.
154. **B** – Handheld cell phone use is prohibited for drivers under 21 and discouraged for all drivers.
155. **B** – If unsure of a sign's meaning, refer to your Missouri Driver Guide.
156. **B** – At an intersection, yield until the vehicle in the intersection has passed.
157. **B** – When children are present at a crossing, slow down and be prepared to stop.
158. **B** – "No Parking" signs mean you cannot park in that designated area.
159. **B** – A "Caution: Winding Road" sign warns you of curves and potential hazards ahead.
160. **B** – To reduce sun glare, use sunglasses and adjust your visor.

This 160-question practice test is designed to cover a broad range of topics relevant to Missouri's driving laws and safe driving practices as of 2025. Review the explanations carefully for any questions you missed, and use this test to reinforce your understanding as you prepare for your permit exam. Good luck, and study hard to pass on your first try!

8.7 TIPS FOR EFFECTIVE STUDYING AND TEST-TAKING

Preparing for the Missouri permit test requires more than just reading through the handbook once and hoping for the best. Understanding the rules of the road, recognising traffic signs, and knowing safe driving practices are all essential, but the way you study and approach the test can make a huge difference in how well you perform. Memorising information without truly understanding it can lead to mistakes, especially when faced with tricky wording or questions designed to test how well you apply what you have learned. Instead of trying to cram everything at the last minute, taking a structured approach and developing strong test-taking strategies will help you retain information more effectively and boost your confidence on test day.

The first step to studying successfully is creating an environment where you can focus without distractions. If you try to study in a noisy place or while multitasking, your brain will struggle to absorb information efficiently. Setting aside dedicated time in a quiet space will help you concentrate, making it easier to retain details about Missouri's traffic laws, road signs, and right-of-way rules. Finding a comfortable study spot—whether it's a desk, a library, or a quiet corner of your home—can make a big difference in how well you engage with the material.

Consistency is another key factor in effective studying. Trying to learn everything in a single session can quickly become overwhelming, and you are more likely to forget what you read if you rush through it. Instead of cramming, breaking your study sessions into shorter, regular intervals helps reinforce the material. Studying a little bit each day allows your brain to process and store information more efficiently. Reviewing one or two topics at a time, such as speed limits or road signs, makes it easier to remember the details compared to trying to absorb everything at once.

Actively engaging with the material instead of passively reading it also makes a big difference. Simply reading through the Missouri Driver Guide without testing your knowledge will not be as effective as using active learning techniques. One helpful method is to summarise information in your own words. After reading about a traffic law or a specific driving rule, try to explain it as if you were teaching someone else. If you can put it into your own words, it means you truly understand it. Writing down key points or making flashcards for difficult concepts can also help reinforce what you learn.

Practice tests are one of the most powerful tools for preparing effectively. Taking multiple practice exams allows you to familiarise yourself with the format of the actual test, helping you feel more comfortable on test day. Missouri's permit test consists of multiple-choice questions, and some of them may include answer choices that seem similar, requiring you to think carefully before selecting the correct response. By working through practice questions, you become better at identifying patterns in how questions are worded and can spot common traps designed to test your understanding. If you get a question wrong, reviewing the correct answer and understanding why you made a mistake will prevent you from repeating the error on the real test.

Spacing out your practice tests over time instead of taking them all at once can further improve your retention. Taking a test after every few study sessions helps reinforce what you have learned while highlighting areas where you need more review. Some online practice tests also track your progress, showing which topics you consistently answer correctly and which ones need more focus.

Understanding road signs is a crucial part of the test, and memorising them through visual association can make recognition much easier. Instead of trying to remember a long list of signs and their meanings all at once, connecting them to real-life situations helps you recall them more naturally. For example, if you see a yellow diamond-shaped sign with a winding arrow, picturing a curvy road in your mind will make it easier to remember that it indicates a winding roadway ahead. Looking for road signs while riding as a passenger or walking near intersections also helps reinforce what they mean. Recognising them in real-life settings strengthens your memory and prepares you for questions that test your ability to identify them on the exam.

As test day approaches, managing test anxiety is just as important as knowing the material. Feeling nervous is completely normal, but letting stress take over can make it harder to concentrate. One way to reduce anxiety is to get plenty of rest the night before the test. Sleep plays a crucial role in memory retention, so staying up late to cram can actually hurt your performance. Reviewing your notes earlier in the day and getting a good night's sleep will leave you feeling more refreshed and alert.

On the day of the test, eating a light meal beforehand can help maintain focus. Skipping breakfast or lunch might leave you feeling tired or distracted, while eating too much heavy food can make you sluggish. Drinking water and avoiding excessive caffeine can also help you stay clear-headed during the exam.

Once you begin the test, pacing yourself is important. Rushing through questions can lead to careless mistakes, while spending too much time on a single question might leave you running out of time. If a question seems difficult, skipping it and returning to it later can prevent you from getting stuck. Many times, other questions on the test may contain clues that help you answer the ones you were unsure about.

Carefully reading each question and all answer choices before selecting your response is critical. Some questions may include answers that are partially correct but not the best choice. Watching out for words like *always*, *never*, and *except* can help you catch tricky wording. If an answer seems obvious but contains an extreme word, reconsidering before selecting it can prevent errors.

After finishing the test, reviewing your answers if time allows can help catch mistakes before submitting it. Sometimes, a second glance at a question might reveal a misinterpretation that you didn't notice the first time.

Approaching the Missouri permit test with confidence comes from proper preparation. Taking the time to study actively, practicing with sample questions, and managing test-day nerves will set you up for success. The more you engage with the material and test your knowledge in different ways, the more prepared you will be when it's time to take the exam.

8.8 ADDITIONAL RESOURCES AND WHERE TO FIND THEM

Finding the right resources can make all the difference when preparing for the Missouri permit test. While studying the official Missouri Driver Guide is essential, relying on a single source of information might not be the most effective way to learn. Expanding your study materials to include a variety of resources will help reinforce key concepts, provide different ways to test your knowledge, and ensure that you are fully prepared for any question that might appear on the test. With Missouri's laws and driving regulations updated periodically, knowing where to access the most current information is just as important as studying itself.

One of the most reliable sources available to you is the **Missouri Department of Revenue (DOR) website**. This official site contains everything you need to know about the permit application process, including updated versions of the Missouri Driver Guide, testing locations, and requirements for obtaining a learner's permit. If there are any changes to state driving laws, this is where you will find them first. Additionally, the website provides information about fees, identification documents needed for applying, and answers to frequently asked questions.

Beyond the official handbook, **online practice tests** are an invaluable tool. Taking practice exams that mimic the format of the real test allows you to become familiar with the types of questions you will encounter. Many websites offer free sample tests, while others provide paid options with additional features like progress tracking and in-depth explanations for every answer. Missouri's permit test includes questions about road signs, traffic laws, and safe driving practices, and taking multiple practice tests helps reinforce this information while highlighting areas where you need to improve.

For a more interactive approach, **mobile apps** designed for Missouri's permit test provide a convenient way to study anywhere. Many apps include flashcards, quizzes, and simulated exams that adjust based on your performance. These apps often break down information into smaller sections, making it easier to digest compared to reading a long handbook in one sitting. Some even send daily notifications with small quiz questions, helping you keep key facts fresh in your mind without overwhelming you. Since laws and test formats can change, choosing an app that specifically focuses on Missouri's permit test rather than a general driving test is essential to ensure you are getting accurate and relevant material.

If you prefer a more structured study method, **driving schools** offer courses that cover all aspects of the permit test. Many driving schools in Missouri provide classroom-based instruction that goes beyond just passing the exam, helping you develop a deeper understanding of road rules and safety. Some schools even offer online courses that allow you to learn at your own pace. While not required for taking the permit test, enrolling in a driving school can be especially helpful if you find it difficult to study on your own or if you want extra guidance before beginning behind-the-wheel training.

For those who learn best through watching and listening, **educational videos** and tutorials can make studying more engaging. Platforms like YouTube have numerous channels dedicated to helping new drivers understand traffic laws, road signs, and test-taking strategies. Some videos explain complex topics with animations, making them easier to grasp compared to reading about them in a book. Watching real-life driving scenarios also helps with visual learning, allowing you to see how certain road situations play out rather than just memorising rules on paper. Since online content varies in accuracy, making sure that the videos you watch are based on Missouri's traffic laws is important to avoid studying incorrect or outdated information.

Another valuable resource that many people overlook is **local libraries**. Most libraries in Missouri have copies of the official Missouri Driver Guide, along with additional books and study materials related to driving laws and road safety. Some libraries also provide access to online databases with permit test resources, allowing you to take practice exams or read digital versions of study guides. If you are looking for a quiet place to study away from distractions, a library can provide an ideal environment to focus on preparing for the test.

For learners who benefit from discussing topics with others, **study groups** can be an effective way to reinforce what you have learned. Studying with friends or family members who are also preparing for the permit test allows you to quiz each other, explain difficult concepts, and discuss road rules in a way that makes the material easier to remember. Even if you are studying alone, asking a parent or experienced driver to go over test questions with you can help clarify any confusion. Some people retain information better when they hear it explained aloud, so having a conversation about Missouri's driving laws instead of just reading them silently might help the details stick more effectively.

As you explore different resources, it is important to ensure that the information you are studying is **current and specific to Missouri**. Some websites, books, and apps provide general permit test information that may not align with Missouri's laws. Checking the publication date of any resource and comparing details with the official Missouri Driver Guide can prevent you from learning outdated or incorrect information. Traffic laws are updated periodically, and what was true a few years ago might no longer apply in 2025.

Since studying for the permit test requires both memorisation and application of knowledge, combining different types of resources can strengthen your understanding and make you feel more prepared. Using a mix of official guides, practice tests, apps, videos, and interactive tools will reinforce what you have learned while making the process more engaging. The more varied your study methods are, the more likely you are to retain important details and apply them correctly when answering test questions.

The Missouri Drivers Permit Study Book 2025

By knowing where to find the best study materials and making use of multiple resources, you can approach the Missouri permit test with confidence. Whether you prefer traditional study methods like reading the handbook or more interactive options like practice tests and videos, having access to reliable information will ensure that you are well-prepared for the test and ready to start your journey as a responsible driver.

Made in the USA
Monee, IL
04 May 2025